IN SEARCH
OF SPIRITUAL
INTELLIGENCE

BETTY STEINHAUER

IN SEARCH OF SPIRITUAL INTELLIGENCE

Published by Woven Word
An Imprint of Fisher King Publishing
The Studio
Arthington Lane
Pool in Wharfedale
LS21 1JZ
England

Cover design from an original concept by Judi Rich
Cover image by Andrew Ostrovsky
Cover photograph of author courtesy of Vicki Mcleod
www.vicmcleod.com

DEDICATION

To all my thirty-nine interviewees who gave so willingly of their thoughts, feelings and time, I am deeply grateful. I have tried my level best to include all your significant thoughts.

To my grandchildren, Spencer, Dawson, Megan and Benjamin, I love you to bits. Ben, I am proud to have quoted you in this book!

To Jody and Julie, my children, I hope one day you will understand me and my love for you a little bit better.

To Dadi Janki, head of the Brahma Kumaris, the very moment I first met you thirty years ago I felt that something had changed in my life… for the better. I look upon you as my mentor. Thank you for teaching me the meaning of strength, toughness, compassion, honesty, bravery. Thank you for showing me how to age. You will be 104 by the time this is published, a razor sharp mind in a very fragile body.

To Judy Johnson, who had me stay in her home for a week and put me in what she called 'writers book camp' every morning, a big thumbs up!

To Gopi Patel, thank you for being my initial inspiration!

To Geeta Agarwal, executive director of Hotel Hillock, Mount Abu, India, thank you for putting me up for two months when I was working on this book. Thank you for offering to host an event to launch this book, which I have accepted with delight.

To the Brahma Kumaris, thank you for sharing your wisdom with me so patiently all these years, thank you for allowing me to enjoy

the hospitality of so many centers. I will admit that the Brahma Kumaris are not a perfect organization (none is, to my mind) but you start from love, truth, respect, kindness, values that are so important to the world.

To all my hosts over the last six years as I travelled the world as a Nomadic Intern, I am grateful beyond words. It hasn't always been perfect but the most wonderful learning anyone could have.

To my friend Paul Knights, who has protected and stored my luggage in Cambridge, UK, and to my friends in Cambridge, you have become one of my heart homes.

To Rick Armstrong, the founder of Fisher King Publishing, who decided over a two-hour lunch that I was worth the risk, my deepest gratitude.

To Charu Bahri, thank you for collaborating with me on this project.

CONTENTS

PREFACE

I was a war baby, born in Luton, UK, in 1943, and raised in Toronto, Canada, where my parents relocated a year or so after armistice. My beginnings were happy enough but soon descended into chaos. When I was barely a teenager I was raped. I was just about recovering from that trauma a couple of years later when I lost my father to a fatal heart attack. My mother subsequently descended into bouts of mental illness so severe, I had to quit high school to support her. But I didn't allow that to keep me down. I picked myself up by the bootstraps. I landed a job as a clerk in the office of the president of a supermarket. I moved on to other jobs as I gained experience. After marrying and having children and losing one, I started to volunteer for community organizations. Over the years I developed a knack for getting things done in the public sector and gradually built a business offering corporations government liaison services, strategic planning and steering their social responsibility initiatives. My consulting firm was called Betty Steinhauer & Associates.

I sure traveled a long way from the other side of the tracks. My early years are testimony to what the spirit can do if you can allow your rational mind to prevail when the going gets tough. But you know what? Intelligence can get you success but it isn't enough to stay happy.

When I lost my baby girl, I also lost faith in God, who had been a source of comfort for me in my childhood. When I walked out of my marriage at the age of forty-three, my relationships with my daughters plummeted to a low. It turned out that I didn't quite have the inner resources, which during the course of writing this book I learned is 'emotional intelligence', to hold onto everyone who was dear to me.

Self-help books and retreats appeased only momentarily. Eventually a power-packed meeting with Dadi Janki, the present head of the Brahma Kumaris, a socio-spiritual organization, and other senior meditation teachers from that group in 1990, and a visit to their headquarters in India set off a deeper engagement with spirituality and started to lengthen the time spans when I felt calm.

If a bigger world view is one of the cornerstones of spirituality, my widening perspective at the outset spurred me to expand the charity work I had begun in Toronto. I founded The People Bridge, an international charity that served communities worldwide, building schools, digging wells, offering healthcare services and filling countless other needs. Mostly, we focused on providing people with the tools and education to motivate themselves.

Over the years, travelling for pleasure and to learn what makes people in distant countries tick led me to realize that people are the same wherever you go, to borrow a line from Paul McCartney. Then why do we draw divisions between Ebony and Ivory? Between East and West? Why aren't we one people?

At the age of sixty-four, I hung up my boots to spend more time understanding the meaning of life. Upon closing my business, I treated myself to a three-month world cruise, during which I began the mammoth task of writing my memoir. I figured the introspection that the process of writing entails would lead me to bigger things. And it did help me realize one fundamental fact about myself. After spending all these years searching the world for a place to call home, I found it in my heart, a place I never knew to look.

My Way was eventually published in 2012. A few months later I was in Toronto crossing a street to deliver a copy of my book to a friend when I was hit by a car. To this day I don't remember a thing except waking up in an ambulance covered in blood and asking the paramedic if I could still make it to my fancy luncheon. He just laughed and told me we were on the way to the hospital. It took my trainer and chiropractor three months to put Humpty Dumpty together again and longer for the wounds on my scalp to heal.

I took the accident as a sign. I felt I had survived for a purpose. What was it?

At the time I lived in the heart of Toronto, in a lovely apartment with all the bells and whistles. I still remember a Saturday when friends were visiting. They said they loved my red couch. On the spur of the moment I said I would sell it to them. Well, we got to chatting and I found myself proposing to give those friends my furniture in return for a place to stay when I was in the city. As the afternoon wore on my thoughts crystallized very naturally. I decided to spend time doing what I loved - and that was travelling the world and experiencing life in different parts. I would travel not as your regular tourist flitting from here to there but as a culture enthusiast spending extended durations in each place I visited. I made up my mind very quickly, it just seemed like the right thing to do, as crazy as that seems. A homeless status didn't bother me one bit. I packed up, gave some of my stuff away, sold some, made my bookkeeper Doreen my power of attorney and felt ready to move on.

In the ensuing months another friend remarked that I was as though interning a nomadic lifestyle. The Nomadic Intern became the name of my blog and in time, the title of the screen adaptation of My Way, which is presently being shopped for production.

My nomadic travels gathered depth last year when I spent some time in Athens with Gopi Patel, a youngish, evolved woman of Indian origin, raised in Africa and the UK, who was at the time teaching Raja Yoga meditation in Greece (nowadays she is travelling the world teaching Raja Yoga meditation). Gopi and I had tea one afternoon, which stretched to dinner because we got so engrossed in chatting about the intelligence quotient, emotional intelligence and spiritual intelligence. We agreed that people are looking for tips to navigate our increasingly chaotic world, they don't want intellectual sermons. We discussed the possibility of me interviewing people to put together a lot of practical advice on spiritual intelligence. Why spiritual intelligence? Looking back on my life, I can clearly see what rational intelligence has done for me and where a lack of emotional intelligence has failed me and how long it has taken me to acquire spiritual intelligence.

Anyway, to get back to that fateful meeting in Athens, after four hours Gopi and I went into a quiet room to reflect on what we had chatted and voila! The very next week I was making a list of potential interviewees. The fact that Athens is where I made great progress in my understanding of spirituality when I spent time there in 2014 with the late Anthony Strano, the best spiritual teacher I ever had, makes me wonder whether the conceptualization of this book was an act of Providence.

So, that is how I ended up interviewing thirty-nine people of all ages and from all walks of life on spiritual intelligence. I met some of those people in my recent travels. Some I have known for years. They are academics, business people, charity workers, doctors, engineers, psychics, writers, artists, religious leaders, and teachers and lifelong practitioners of meditation. Though they may differ greatly from one another, I chose them based on two commonalities - their humanity and humility.

May I also mention here the Reverend Georgie Baxendale from Glasgow, Scotland, who I have known for some years, and who I wanted to interview for this project but who was unable to give me time because of her poor health. Georgie is a fighter and her love for God is so resolute that she makes an impact wherever she goes. I know her amazing spirit has deeply touched me. Hats off to you, Georgie girl!

Coming back to this book, I asked each of my interviewees what they believe spiritual intelligence is and what it means to them, how it is relevant to each of us individually and to the world as a whole in these turbulent times, and, based on their experience, how they each developed spiritual intelligence.

My wish for In Search of Spiritual Intelligence is to reveal wisdom that can help you and me become the best version of ourselves, and discover ways to add value to our lives and to today's fast-paced world. I sincerely hope I have served as the bridge to ideas from across the world.

Ultimately, In Search of Spiritual Intelligence does not strive to be an intellectual book; rather, it focuses on stories about each subject's personal journey on their own spiritual path with the aim of giving its readers a path to their own spiritual intelligence.

I used to be considered crazy for my interest in spirituality but no longer. Why?

I first travelled to India in 1991, to attend a spiritual retreat. My friends thought I was crazy to want to learn how to meditate. Since then, I have revisited the country every couple of years, and in recent years, practically every year. Between then and now, something major has changed.

People no longer think I'm crazy to want to learn (yes, I'm still learning, it takes forever) how to meditate. Some of my friends actually ask me what sort of meditation I practice. Others who aren't interested in meditation themselves are still respectful of my position.

I'm not the only one to have felt a shift in people's perceptions to meditation and, in general, to conversations about spirituality (as opposed to organized religion). Jayanti Kirpalani, who is the European Director of the Brahma Kumaris, told me she has seen a 'spiritual awakening' of sorts in the last decade.

Jayanti has been travelling the world to share ideas on spirituality since forty years. I've known her for the last three decades.

In the eighties and nineties, Jayanti said, she used to get asked very challenging questions about spirituality. A few people used to be dismissive or even sarcastic during talks. She doesn't get that any more. To the contrary, since 2008 or so, she has been increasingly asked questions of personal inquiry by people who sincerely want to know what's going on inside themselves and to learn how to deal with the situations they find themselves in. She has found these people very open to learn.

Jayanti sees this change as happening across the world, more so in South America and Australia, and to a lesser extent, in North America, and in places like East Europe and Russia. Forty years ago, she said, younger people used to be asking questions about spirituality. Today, the curiosity spans people of all ages and backgrounds. The establishment, especially in Europe, has also become more accepting of meditation. A case in point - last year Jayanti was asked to lead meditation at Davos, the annual meeting of the World Economic Forum, an event that brings together the who's who of the political and business world and of late, environment thought leaders. As I see it, that's a huge indication of how acceptable meditation has become to the establishment.

When I was researching this project, I came across a Wiki entry on spiritual intelligence. It told me that in 1997, Ken O'Donnell, an Australian author and consultant living in Brazil, had introduced the term 'spiritual intelligence' in his Portuguese book Endoquality, a term symbolizing the emotional and spiritual dimensions of human beings in organizations. I was aware that Ken was a senior Raja Yoga meditation practitioner with the Brahma Kumaris, and also the coordinator of their thirty or so centers in South America. However, I did not know Ken personally as I know many seniors of that institution. Still, just seeing his name on that Wiki page almost caused me to back out of this project. What could I possibly add to the available literature on spiritual intelligence when someone with close to half a century's experience in meditation had already written reams on it?

Eventually, I was talked back into the project, so to speak, and actually went on to interview Ken for this book.

When he spoke, he told me something that affirmed Jayanti's view on the greater acceptance of meditation, if not spirituality, in South America.

"I was recently in Argentina meeting with five or six Congressmen and women who were interested in meditation," he said. "We were in the Congress building where they meet dignitaries and I thought this would never have happened a decade or two ago when I started to write about these things."

Ken told me his first book on spirituality at the workplace was the 1991 publication The Soul in Business.

"Everyone laughed at it when it was released," he said. "But you know what, that early pioneer had its uses. A few months ago the program director of a leading business school in Brazil got in touch with me and asked me to conduct some courses. I was curious to know how she had heard of me, and asked her. And she referred to that book and said, 'You used to write about these things and now we realize that we need to learn them and put them in practice.'"

"Wow!" I said, with a chuckle. "I love it when things come full circle!"

I'd like to quote Upkar Arora here. Upkar is a successful business man, a family man and a deep thinker, who I call a friend. We met around fifteen years ago when we both sat on the board of an art gallery in Toronto, where he lives. We have stayed in touch since, catching up whenever I am in the city.

"I see a heightened sense of self consciousness and universal consciousness today, more than I have certainly seen in thirty years," he said.

Upkar attributed some of this change to influences from the East such as meditation and Buddhism.

I don't want to complicate this chapter by introducing more of my respondents but let me just say that many of those I interviewed shared this observation. Here are some of the comments that were made:

I find it easier to have conversations about spirituality with people. Today even a delivery man may have heard of 'mindfulness' and knows that it is a technique that could help him focus and work better and faster.

Some years back we needed to word spirituality differently. Now people are more open to any type of spirituality. Today I see people meditating silently in squares and plazas. This interest allows those who have been meditating since many years to share more.

I see a huge number of people who are trying to invest in a new kind of wisdom, which you could call spiritual intelligence.

Young people are looking for some learning that they aren't getting in schools, a new perception of everything.

So, what is getting people to start thinking?

Having interviewed a considerable number of spiritually aware people from all walks of life for this book, I have come to the conclusion that two societal changes are triggering this shift. On the one hand, life is getting harder and more uncertain. And on the other hand, we have moved away from God and our community networks have weakened, leaving us with fewer of the traditional supports that we used to rely on to tide over challenging life situations.

When my children were growing up, we didn't have social media nor cable channels. We used to send kids out to play and say, 'Come home when the street lights come on'. They'd run around, ride their bikes or whatever. You didn't worry; they would always show up for meals.

A few years ago I was babysitting my grandchildren and my daughter made me promise not to leave them by themselves - not even for a minute - even though we were playing on the front steps or in the front yard. What a different set of rules! The pity is fear underlies these rules.

"The basic underlying mood is one of panic," said Samuel Kimbriel, a friend and an incredibly bright young philosopher who is involved in building high level think tank projects in Washington and the west coast of USA. "People are afraid," he said.

"I live in daily fear about the state of the world," said Kathy Barrett, a special friend.

I've known Kathy since 2012. We were introduced by a common acquaintance and thereafter she attended the first Spirit of Humanity forum in Iceland as my guest. Kathy is a successful writer living in Woodstock, a wooded town in upstate New York best known for the famous music festival held near it in 1969. What strikes me most about her is her natural spirituality. She is spiritual without being part of any formal spiritual group.

Kathy narrated feeling locked up in a 'self-imposed prison of misery' when she watches or reads the news, goes on twitter or witnesses the actions of President Trump. "I feel helpless to initiate change and the more I inform and educate myself about what is happening, the less hopeful I become," she said.

I could relate to what she said. When I was younger we were very well integrated with our immediate communities. We had some idea of world events but we didn't have the world in our faces all the time. Today, many of us don't know our neighbors let alone how they are doing, but we are clued in with the rest of the world. And it is a rapidly changing world, with a culture that is rapidly disintegrating. It is scary to see everything you believe in unravel in front of your eyes.

"Listening to the news gets more and more difficult," said Michael Levine, a true friend for thirty-five years and a retired professor of political science in the US, when I asked him why he thought spiritual intelligence might be relevant to our lives.

I couldn't agree more. I wake up in the morning and turn on the news not just for information but to hear if any disaster-like event has happened in the world, where I am or where I plan to be, or that I need to be aware of. I am relieved when things seem to be normal, when there are no shocks to deal with.

I know of people who point to recent technological developments and use these as props to believe that the world is becoming a better place to live in. So we're building taller. We're flying faster. We're reaching further out in space. But I'm sure we don't live in a gentler society.

If I may quote Brahma Kumar Nirwair here - he is one of the very senior members of the Brahma Kumaris in its Mount Abu headquarters, although I would prefer to introduce him as the most gracious man I've ever known. He has been practicing meditation since sixty years; I've known him for thirty years.

When I interviewed Nirwair for this project of mine, I asked him what he thought was bringing about the shift in people's perception. He said, "all the emphasis in the last few centuries has been on material improvement, material development," and he then correlated material development with temporary happiness... the happiness you get from acquiring something, which doesn't stay with you. It fades away. And then you want to experience it again, and your desire shifts to another thing, and you feel happy when you obtain that. And then it is a third thing... and so on. In this never-ending quest eventually you become exhausted.

"So what do you think people are becoming conscious of now?" I asked him.

"Character and the environment," said Nirwair.

Essentially, he said, people have started to look inward. He felt that people have grown aware to the shift in society, or as he put it, to the fact that, "the world is totally different to what it was when I was growing up."

He described the middle class environment he grew up in, in a village in Punjab, in north India, which I shall narrate for a reason.

"Every family had enough land. Every family owned enough cattle. It was a loving environment. Everyone trusted everyone else.

It was unheard of to lock your home. If at all the doors were bolted, it was only to keep out stray cats and dogs. People were really happy. We had one drunk in the whole village of 150 families. No one else touched alcohol. Elders had love for children and children respected their elders for their character and high thinking. We were brought up in a virtuous environment. Our elders instilled values in us by example. I vividly remember my grandfather. He would get up very early morning and recite the entire holy book of the Sikhs. He wouldn't involve himself in unnecessary discussion and so, his words were highly valued. He lived to 103 years and he never needed medicine. He worked in the fields until the end. When he died the villagers celebrated his life. They played music along his funeral procession, showering people with dry fruit and currency."

Over in the West, I can't say I had it as good as Nirwair did in my childhood. I lost my father young and had to deal with a mother who had psychological issues, but still, the broader environment I lived in worked, so to speak.

Today, nothing works the way it is meant to. You can't take anything or anyone for granted anymore, and that has dealt a blow to the concept of security that we grew up with.

In my travels, I have felt the sense of panic that Samuel spoke of, in people across the world, a helplessness I identify with. We are seeking to make sense of the increasingly crazy world we live in.

Samuel made an interesting point. He said, "I think these conditions of fear and difficulty will press people to ask questions more seriously than they would have otherwise. You know, Christ says the kingdom of heaven is like a treasure hidden in a field. I think some of those who search will end up finding the treasure. And they will want to make the deep sacrifices to hold on to it and not let it go for anything. So if the crisis of the world precipitates the ability in some people to build their lives out of stone instead of sand, that seems worth it, according to me."

They say every cloud has a silver lining.

I can affirm that the situations I have faced in my life and what I see happening in the world have spurred me to question my life and the world. Of late, I have been thinking deeply about spiritual intelligence. And so, was born this book, In Search of Spiritual Intelligence.

In Search of Spiritual Intelligence is my quest to understand spiritual intelligence, and explore whether spirituality (and spiritual intelligence, as its expression) is the missing dimension of our lives - both from the perspective of being a factor to help us live in these times of uncertainty, and, whether its scarcity is the reason for our disintegrating world.

I can assure you of one thing. The wisdom I came upon is sure to help me navigate what's left of my life. It will help me find peace and contentment no matter what situation I may find myself in. It will help me feel compassion notwithstanding what befalls me. It will help me stay strong in the face of adversity. And since spirituality seems to have become more acceptable - quite the buzzword - it may resonate with you too.

*

I have divided this book in seven parts. Part one aims at shedding some light on the self. Understanding the self is a prerequisite to working on the self. Then I introduce spiritual intelligence. Understanding God comes next, and then I write on making sense of the world we live in and navigating our way through tough situations. I then get into the nitty-gritty details of applying spirituality to life and touch upon several aspects that a seeker needs to think about - the spiritual journey, diet, lifestyle, spiritual mentorship, taking responsibility for your initiatives and so on. Lastly, I close with a few thoughts on why a spiritual perspective is the only way forward.

PART ONE

You are not your ego

I first met Neville Hodgkinson in the early nineties, in UK, just prior to my first visit to India. Neville is a medical and science writer, as bright as they come. He has a clear intellect and a questioning mind, as you might expect from a correspondent. That said, one of the things that struck me when I got to know Neville was that he never seemed to be comfortable in his skin. He seemed happy but a certain comfort was missing.

A few years ago, I sensed that something had changed in Neville's life. He seemed more relaxed and if I may say so, he started to reflect an easier spiritual vibe. I never got around to asking him what had happened and even when I sat down to interview him for this initiative I wasn't quite sure if I would get to hear what had brought about the change in him.

One of the questions I asked all my interviewees was to share a valuable episode from their spiritual journey. Well, guess what? Neville chose to talk about the life-altering experience that helped him acquire a sense of ease that you usually associate with a person who is very comfortable with his role in the world, which gave him the ability to interact and engage with the world with greater impact.

"When I began to practice Raja Yoga meditation (with the Brahma Kumaris) in 1981, my children were aged eleven and twelve. I had a family life. I was working hard as a journalist. My wife Liz was also a journalist.

"Some seven to eight years after I had been practicing meditation, when my elder son Tom was in university and Will, the younger one was about to go to university, Liz (now my ex) said that she wanted us to separate because she wasn't really interested in what I was interested in. She didn't say that but she said, we met young, we married young, we had a family young, she had never lived as a single woman, and she wanted to experience that. So that was a polite way of saying get out."

I chuckled. "How did you feel about that?" I asked.

"I was quite reluctant. Parting seemed the right thing to do in the sense that that was what she wanted, and I was always taught to not be selfish. If you love someone then you want to give them what they want. And so, anyway, the marriage ended.

"We had a very beautiful house which we had to sell. We split the proceeds. Liz took a bit more so that she could take a bigger place so she could continue to look after our sons when they came home from university. And life moved on.

"I poured myself into my work. I would see my ex and my sons fairly regularly but more or less we were going our different ways. This went on for years. And when I did link with them, I would feel a sense of loss. It would kind of remind me that I had lost a lot, in terms of the comfort of family life and relationships. It wasn't very conscious but I would lose myself with them, and then when I was back in my non family context I would feel a sort of hollow. For two to three days it would disturb me. And this went on for years until eventually, about five or six years back I realized that there was this family man identity in my ego that I hadn't let go."

"Ego?", I asked.

"Well, you can call it a persona," said Neville. "Psychologists tell us that you need an ego, a sense of identity, to function. And it is true, in the same way as we are embodied souls, we need a body to play these parts in life, you need an ego, which is a limited sense of identity, to engage with the world."

"What were some of the egos you used to engage with the world?" I asked.

"I am a journalist. I am a family man. I am a father. I am a grandfather. And so on."

"Okay. And those weren't all a problem?"

"No. I was playing many roles without over-identifying with them, while staying focused on my true identity, the spirit within. Only my family man identity was a problem. A limited identity becomes a problem only if we grow too attached to it; because then it shifts the focus away from what is real, the spirit within. In neglecting the true identity and staying focused only on the illusion, the external identity that is here today and gone tomorrow, we experience pain when we finally have to give up the limited identity, such as when we resign from a job or when we part ways with a partner or at the end of a lifetime. I had ceased to be a family man many years ago but I was still hurting at the loss of that ego role."

"And how was that hurting holding back your spiritual progress?"

"Well, my true identity, the soul is an energy that is benevolent, peaceful and full of love. The soul doesn't buy into social structures. It isn't built into it that it has to be a family man. But by being caught up in my limited identity of being a family man, the lightness of being that is so beautiful for the soul, sometimes I would be getting it, and sometimes I would be losing it. I couldn't enjoy that lightness every moment, at will."

"What happened next?"

"When I realized what was going on I envisaged my family man identity like a tumor in my brain that was infiltrating my thinking in a variety of ways, not just that one I have described, and was holding me back on my spiritual journey. It is an odd thing. I am not taken to visualizations and things but on this occasion I saw this sort of gray thing with tentacles spreading through my brain. It was affecting my thinking quite widely, where this attachment and dependency remained."

"So did you get rid of the persona?"

"I put my hand on my head and I pulled out tumor, so to speak! The proof that it came out was in the aftereffects. I hurt a bit for some time, the ego inflamed. You could say I was in recovery. But a little while afterwards, when it settled, I felt really free."

"Do you feel better now?"

"Of course. I feel free not only to move forward on my spiritual journey but also to stride forward in my own spiritual intelligence. And the thing is, when we progress spiritually, it is good for everyone around us. A consequence of my freedom is that I have come closer to those family members with who I have a special relationship. My relationship with them is no longer one of neediness, and dependency or hurt when there is loss, instead of that there is just a desire to give and share happiness when we come together. Now that is so different."

I was curious about one aspect. "Did rustling up the courage to free yourself of this weight in the mind affect your physical self in any way," I asked Neville.

"Yes, it did," he said. "I mentioned the lightness of being that I was sometimes getting and sometimes missing. After this episode I felt much better physically as well. In fact, this experience left me in no doubt that there is no limit to what the soul can do to change the brain and the body. It just takes a really powerful will to do it."

"Is that scientifically proven, Neville, or just faith speaking?" I asked.

"It's scientifically proven, Betty," he clarified. "Normally we consider the body to be a pretty stable affair. But ultimately the mind is in charge and if you make a change of mind, the body of course will change. This is now confirmed by the concept of neuroplasticity and how the brain rewires itself depending on how you use it."

Neville spoke with such humility it left me in no doubt that this man, this soul, was no longer under the influence of any of his limited identities. I felt privileged to have heard his story and to have him as a friend.

*

One of my key takeaways from Neville's sharing was that the more we can identify with our real identity, the spirit within, the easier it should be to die.

Don't get me wrong, I'm not morose about the idea of dying. Not in the least bit. I'm personally very comfortable with facing my own end.

During my conversation with Samuel, I said to him that if someone were to diagnose me with terminal cancer, I'd be absolutely fine. I would never have chemo. I would just get on a plane and run around the world seeing the people I wanted to see and then die. But you know what? When I say this to people, they get uncomfortable.

Samuel nodded wisely and put down such behavior to our living in a culture that is continuously fleeing death. "We're clinging to life," he explained. "You can see this pretty clearly if you go to hospices and talk to people who work with end of life situations. Sometimes the people who are dying are pretty at ease with letting their lives go. But their families and the people around them are desperately clinging to ways to keep them alive. I think that is endemic to the culture we live in. Its basic infrastructure is built around protecting and insulating us from loss and death."

"Hasn't humanity always been like that?" I asked.

"The ancient world was built totally differently," Samuel continued. "Did you know that Socrates said that the purpose of life is to learn how to die well?"

"I hadn't heard that," I said. "That's deep."

"Yes. The ancients sought to live in coherence with the highest identity. Not that there weren't problems in that culture. It was a culture that was frivolous with many people's lives. Slaves, a lot of women and children were worthless so it didn't matter how they were treated. But I think they did see clearly that living a life under the tyranny of the fear of death was not worthwhile."

"That's interesting," I said. "Socrates lived in around 400 BC. Over two millennia later, women and children are still vulnerable sections of society. But we have come a long way away from being in tune with the idea of dying. Our personas have become the be all and end all of our existence. Is it time to change that perspective?"

I love how Pilar Quera, a meditation teacher based in Barcelona, who I befriended many years ago when I attended a retreat in Spain, described the outcome of our preoccupation with labels, or personas.

She said, "By labeling humanity, we have forgotten what defines us as human beings. We are living visibly as humans without feeling the force of being, the divine."

Living without the force of being - I am pretty certain that isn't a life worth living.

Question, question, question

In the last chapter, Neville spoke of freeing himself from a persistently troubling aspect of ego, so as to be better able to focus on the truth. Neville has been meditating since decades, and so, he was able to draw on an inner reservoir of energy finally to shrug off this particular burden. I've dabbled with spirituality since decades too, but still felt that I needed to go deeper into the actual process of getting to the truth.

The truth is the spirit within. What I wanted to know was how do you develop an awareness of the truth such that it never leaves you? It becomes you.

The best answer came from my scholarly friend Samuel. He quoted the wisdom of ancient Greek philosophers, who believed one of the main goals of life was to see the truth, to see reality, and they equated this truth with God or their pantheon of Gods.

"Well," I said. "That's just what I was asking" (although I don't think that puts me on the same level as Greek philosophers!).

"Centuries ago the Oracle of Delphi delivered the command 'know thyself'," started Sam. "Socrates agreed and so advised 'cultivate the self'."

"The ancients believed that inherent impurities keep the self from seeing the truth, or purity, or the divinity which shapes everything. And so, they committed themselves to fostering the inner world, that is, to cultivate the self to try to become pure as the purest objects are pure, until they successfully awaken the intellectus, the higher part of the mind (as opposed to ratio, the lower part of the mind), which is precisely that center of awake-ness or awareness that sees what is actually there."

"How did they do that?" I asked.

"The ancients believed that mysticism paved the road to self evolution," he said.

Now Sam blows me away with his wisdom (he has a doctoral degree from Cambridge and has won various academic awards), but mysticism was kind of heavy duty.

"Mysticism," I asked, somewhat incredulously. "Isn't that asking for too much from people who aren't used to thinking about serious stuff? I can't see myself as a mystic," I added for good measure.

Samuel agreed that mysticism is a word, and indeed, a practice that many would shy away from today, but that, he said, was only because we do not understand what it is and what benefit it brings.

"Let me give you an example to explain," he said. "You know the word theory?"

"Theory," I said. "That means a concept or hypothesis, right?"

"That is the modern perception of the word theory," he said. In the modern world, if I were to describe a theory to you, you would accept the information through your senses, build up a model in your head, and if that model were to correspond to what you see outside, you would accept it as true, and if it didn't, you would call out my theory as false."

"I suppose that is correct," I wondered what he was getting at.

"But in ancient Greek, the word theoria means mystical encounter or contemplation. It is derived from a verb which means to look, or to see. It means bringing out your own self, putting it on the line and going through the process to come face to face with what is deeply real."

"So, in other words, to theorize means to question every single belief, contemplate, and discard what is not real," I asked.

"Precisely," he said. "And that is why mysticism is at the heart of intellectual tradition. We would not have medical or scientific or literary or philosophical traditions without mysticism. For the ancients, mysticism is the key to having an encounter with the highest part of reality, and through that, to becoming spiritually intelligent."

"So would you say mysticism is a tool to develop oneself?"

"It is a tool to foster the internal world but it is worth considering that inner development is also external, in the sense that it is coming to see the divine objects which shape everything."

"That's fascinating," I said. "You know, most people think of mysticism as something magical, something no one quite knows what it is. Don't you also think that people are scared of mysticism?"

"Yes. In the early modern period, people have given up on the task of cultivating (or purifying) the self in order to get to the external, and instead they try to go directly, and so we have ended up with a culture that is not just afraid of but also deeply resistant to mysticism. The thing is, in trying to avoid mysticism we have ended up living in an unreal world."

"The ancient Greeks were cautious about what they accepted as true," I remarked.

"Absolutely," he said. "And not just them, philosophers for a good 1,800 years or so, made questioning their beliefs the norm. It isn't easy, it takes courage, but it is how you move towards greater awareness."

I thought a lot about what Samuel had said. His explanations somehow reminded me of something Upkar said when I interviewed him for this book.

Upkar was raised in the early seventies in a very racist society in London, Ontario, Canada. He went to a high school with 2,600 young people who were 99% white. In conversation with me, he summarized his school experience as follows - "I was seen as an outsider in that community and so I experienced all sorts of bullying."

Upkar suffered considerably as a result of his circumstances. "I had few friends and felt isolated and lonely and depressed. My parents were trying to settle in as new immigrants so there was no great support on that front. I had a lot of time to think about stuff."

Upkar realized that people's religious beliefs were impeding instead of contributing to societal harmony. Therefore, there must be something very seriously wrong with religion.

Thinking soon turned into questioning.

"I refused to accept anything at face value," he said.

Questioning and rationalizing and discarding, again and again, led Upkar to shun the hypocrisy of formal religiosity that in his case, and for so many of us, 'is rammed down our throats'.

A Sikh by birth, he gradually went on to reject organized religion and formed his own views on core values to live by. As he said, "Questioning and exploration helped me develop a set of spiritual principles. I drew my own conclusions of what is real and what isn't."

"So what is real for you?" I asked.

Upkar smiled. "A sense of compassion for all and helping others," he said.

Upkar's practice of questioning extended to every sphere of his life including the workplace. "I questioned the definition of success that society bestows on us, and gradually moved away from equating success with money, titles, stature and material possessions."

"So how did you define success?"

"Success to me is the synchronicity of heart, mind, body and spirit, and having the freedom to choose."

I thought of Upkar's experience in the light of Sam's description of the way to get to the truth. It made a lot of sense. I realized that even today people who are serious about awakening own the practice of contemplation and questioning.

I'd like to narrate a story from Anthony D'Mello's much loved book of shorts, The Song of The Bird. [D'Mello was an Indian Jesuit priest and spiritual teacher].

The story is called, The Truth Shop.

I could hardly believe my eyes when I saw the name of the shop: The Truth Shop.

The salesgirl was very polite: What type of truth did I wish to purchase, partial or whole? The whole truth, of course. No deceptions for me, no defenses, no rationalizations.

I wanted my truth plain and unadulterated. She waved me on to another side of the store.

The salesman there pointed to the price tag. "The price is very high, Sir," he said.

"What is it?" I asked, determined to get the whole truth, no matter what it cost. "Your security, Sir," he answered.

I came away with a heavy heart. I still need the safety of my unquestioned beliefs.

*

Jayanti, who has been on the spiritual path for over forty years, expressed the need for ongoing questioning and to be honest with yourself if you want to continue to evolve.

"You read something, somebody tells you something, you see something," she said. "We are exposed to so many influences that continuous inner checks are a must to stay aware of what is real and what is illusion."

What does it mean to be a free thinker? And why is it essential?

A friend of mine in Great Britain, David Goodman, worked as a children's dentist until he retired. Now he indulges his love for meditation and sports.

I first met David in 1990 on my maiden visit to India as a guest of the Brahma Kumaris, a socio-spiritual organization he is associated with. What strikes me the most about the time I've spent with him over the last thirty years is that he is great company. David has a cool sense of humor, he is fun to be around, we strike up great conversations and I appreciate his rebellious streak, which is not to say that he lacks discipline.

David committed himself to the fairly strict lifestyle endorsed by members of the Brahma Kumaris at the age of twenty-four (he is around sixty now). The thing is, I know plenty of people within the Brahma Kumaris, and they all aren't as easy and interesting to be around. What stands out about David, and others who I am comfortable with, is that they are open to different viewpoints. David often quotes spiritual masters from outside the organization he belongs to, to explain a point, which makes for much richer explanations. His openness is rooted in his understanding of spiritual intelligence.

When I asked David what spiritual intelligence means to him, he emphasized the ability to think freely.

"I don't do second-hand thinking," he said.

I found that intriguing. "What do you mean by that?" I asked.

David explained the need to always think things through. Even if someone asks you to follow a rule, make sense of it before you own it.

In a previous chapter, some of my interviewees said that the way to make spiritual progress is to keep questioning your beliefs until you get to the truth. Free thinking is ingrained in questioning in the sense that if you already have an answer in your head, you're not going to be able to answer any question honestly.

Free thinking means you are open to any answer. Now here's the thing. To think freely, you must not be weighed down by your past thought patterns or habits. You must be living in the moment.

To drive home this point, David made a reference to the Indian philosopher Jiddu Krishnamurti's concept of listening.

"Krishnamurti would ask people, 'How do you listen?' His premise was that the mind has desires, fears, hopes and anxieties that tend to influence how we engage with the world, including what we listen to, such that we end up listening only to what we want to hear - in effect, to what gives us satisfaction and comfort, while unthinkingly discarding thoughts and ideas that don't fit into our world view. However, to truly catch what is being said to us, including the feeling behind words spoken to us, and to truly know what is happening around, to engage with the world meaningfully, we need to listen without filters. We need to quiet the mind, that is, free it of the hopes, desires, fears and so on that speak to it unendingly, wastefully so, because all those emotions are a burden of the past. Krishnamurti said true listening is eternal because it is neither of time nor of the mind."

"That sounds profound," I said. "If I might clarify a practical aspect, say I am in bondage to my desires, hopes, fears, anxieties and so on, how might I lose out?"

"A free thinker can think out-of-the-box when a situation comes up. Anyone else will respond to a situation by default, as they always have in the past. And that response may not be good enough," he said. "How we respond to a situation can spell the difference between overcoming it and losing to it."

"That sounds tough," I said.

"I'll give you an example. In the military, you're trained to obey. When a superior says dive left, you go left. If you don't move when you're told to, you're dead. Essentially, the military trains you to the point where you don't think. Likewise, some people can only function in a set pattern.

"Now the challenge is that we live in a world that is changing so fast and that is getting so demanding to live in that if you can't think freely, let alone think, you may not be able to deal with an adverse situation. To continue with the same example of the military, imagine if you were used to diving left every time your superior called out and even if he didn't, just by habit. And then a time came when you needed to turn right. How would you know that you needed to turn right? A free thinker would catch the signal to do things differently because the situation had changed. But someone whose mind was already full of stuff would not. Until you can quiet the noise in your mind, until you can still your mind, until you can free it from meaningless projections, you can't really listen nor can you think freely."

"So, what you're saying is that a free mind can think freely, and unless we can think freely, we can't always take the right decisions."

"Yes. And it isn't just taking decisions for you," David said. "In the challenging times we live in, people will look to someone who they see as being connected for assistance. It helps the world to become spiritually streetwise, if I may put it that way."

I liked that idea.

"Can you give me an example of someone whose mind is free?"

"For me, Dadi Janki (the present head of the Brahma Kumaris) is in a state where she captures signs. She very easily does things differently, and she thinks fast. If she's got a thought to ring Betty she'll ask her assistant to call you now. She won't wait five minutes."

"Why is the time in which we respond important?" I asked.

"I've just read a very interesting book called The Five Second Rule by Mel Robbins. One of the things I learned was that our brains are wired in a way that if we get a thought, we have five seconds to do something about it before the mind and the brain talk us out of it. So, it's not only important to catch what you need to do but also to act on it promptly."

The need to think and act swiftly and precisely came up in conversation with Ken.

I have introduced Ken as an author and experienced meditation teacher. I should also say that he started his career as an industrial chemist, and worked in quality control, processes, organizational development and leadership development. Over five decades, he has delivered over a thousand talks in Australia, India, USA, Europe and Latin America on stress management, positive consciousness, motivation, conflict resolution and other subjects.

Ken told me that someone in one of Europe's biggest banks had gotten in touch with him not so long ago about a course for high performing teams that he had developed for a huge Spanish telecommunications company employing 350,000 people around the world. The banker had wanted Ken to adapt that course for bank employees.

Ken asked the banker what problem the bank was facing. His response was, "We are finding it difficult to compete with virtual banks. They can offer their customers better rates because they don't have overheads."

"What did you reply?" I asked.

"I told him I couldn't help him to compete with the virtual world. But I would be able to help the bank to compete with other banks like itself; other bricks-n-mortar establishments."

Ken went on to explain to the banker that to be better in today's world you need to be able to think better, smarter and quicker.

"You need people with skills to assess situations quickly and make snap judgments on the factors that need to be worked on," he explained. "That necessitates a perception of the big picture. You need people who can cut through the confusion and get to the core. Today you can't survive with 100,000 thoughts every day, of which 90% are waste. You need people who can redirect their thinking to what matters. That necessitates mental agility. Eventually I made the connection between those skills and being in tune with oneself and the world."

"At the end of the day, aren't those the same skills that help people succeed in life?" I asked.

"Sure," said Ken. "In business, in negotiating a career, in managing a family or simply moving up in life you need a better relationship with yourself."

Aim to make your life more meaningful

I can't say enough about the need to question. The thing is, the idea of questioning disturbs some people. I don't think it is so much the questioning as the thought that if they realize that something is amiss, they would need to do something about it. And that something may mean changing their life. And change is a pain for people who are stuck in a comfort zone.

For that reason, I would like to present the thinking of a friend who picked up a cue to reflect from an innocent episode in her life. Reflection is nothing but questioning, and in the case of Briony Bax, a trained actress who works as the editor of Ambit, a British literary and arts magazine with a global audience, questioning changed the course of her life.

It wasn't as if Briony became spiritually oriented or anything similar. No. Briony thinks spirituality is a lot of hog wash!

So why did I interview her for a book on spirituality?

Simply because I think the process is more important than where it gets you. It is important to question. If your questioning is honest - as was hers - whatever happens next will be good.

First, a few words from Briony on what set her thinking -

"Briony, tell me about the episode that changed your life?" I prompted.

For the record, the episode you are about to read, happened before I got to know her. Briony and I met about ten years ago through a mutual friend, and clicked instantly.

"Back in 2007, I was sitting in my beautiful home in Piedmont, California, when I opened a letter asking my family to support the construction of a home for displaced and abandoned children in Gilgil, Kenya," she started.

"In the letter, my Auntie Anne described her endeavor to raise money for a building project. She and her friend Jill Simpson had completed a 'Granny Walk', a 165 km trek across the Turkana desert to raise money. The Turkana is not just any desert, it is known for its winds, desolation and remoteness. An accompanying photograph showed both the grannies in their Liberty print cotton dresses and wide brimmed hats. The letter got me thinking.

"I thought about how I was spending the month. My children were in high school and thinking about college. My husband was away a lot setting up his new business. I was attending school events, golfing, cooking and writing the occasional poem. Then I thought about how the grannies had spent their time, sleeping out in the open air, digging for water, facing sandstorms. I resolved to help them."

"Did the idea of helping people kindle something in you?" I asked.

"It wasn't as if I had never helped people. I had spent many years helping young people in shelters for the homeless, in schools and working at Planned Parenthood. I think receiving the letter from my aunt opened up a whole world of possibilities. Also, it reminded me of my own childhood. My father left when I was six months old. My mum, a single working mother with three children, was often absent. I was the 'scholarship' child at school. I understood what it is to feel alone."

I nodded. I'd been in that space after my father died when I was in my teens.

"I'd always wanted to help charities in East Africa but I didn't trust the big NGOs with their huge advertising budgets," she continued. "So, I decided to set up a charity myself. That is how The Orphan Support League came about. That summer my family visited East Africa and Saidia for the first time."

In Briony's case, reflection redefined how she would spend her energy. Helping orphaned children attend university or vocational school and find a place in the world has brought a lot of happiness and satisfaction in her life. It has helped her bring into effect what she sees as the purpose of life - 'leaving the world a better place than you found it' - a purpose which is spiritual to my mind (even if she would not agree) because helping from the heart is rooted in a vision sans boundaries, and if that isn't spirituality then I don't know what is.

"We can all effect change to make the world a better place," said Briony. "If ever I feel overwhelmed or despondent I look at a quote I have pasted on my computer, by the pilot, Betty Reese. It goes 'If you think you are too small to be effective, you have never been in bed with a mosquito'."

*

While working on this project, I had the privilege to hear from a man who had the world at his feet, so to speak, but who still chose the unconventional path, I reckon, because it had heart.

That man is William Storrar, a minister of the Church of Scotland and director of the Center of Theological Inquiry in Princeton NJ, USA. I first met Will, as his friends call him, five years ago at the Spirit of Humanity forum in Iceland. He invited me to attend a residential conference at Windsor Castle, which was an amazing experience, and later hosted me when I visited Scotland.

William's was one of the first names I listed when I started to identify the people I would interview for this project.

He studied politics in the University of Edinburgh in the early 1970s, and thereafter spent a couple of years working in post graduate studies in politics. At the age of twenty-two, William ran the campaign for the distinctive position of Rector of the university, for a well-known public figure in Britain from Scotland. He ran a brilliant campaign and his candidate won by a landslide despite standing against the political machine of Gordon Brown (later prime minister), the retiring student Rector.

The Rector chairs the governing body of the university. When his candidate won, William was appointed the Rector's Assessor to represent him in university life and serve alongside the Rector on the governing body. In the euphoric moments following that victory, William recollected someone saying, "You can go anywhere now, the world is at your feet", in the context of the power and influence he had gained from his campaign success and prestigious university appointment.

But instead of feeling upbeat about the win, William said, "I had the unsettling experience of not finding the power and influence I had gained fulfilling.

"I felt a kind of disturbance that I had to test. In our church tradition we do that with the support of our local church minister by going to a selection school for a few days and exploring a possible vocation to the ordained ministry."

"Wow," I said. "Were you ready for that call?"

"Well, I had been profoundly nurtured in the Christian faith by my mother. I always had a sense of God, a relationship with God. I had become more involved as a student with the student Christian society and church life. I had self awareness. I had been a high school debater. I had abilities to communicate. I had concern for people and genuinely enjoyed interacting with people.

"Having said that, I had a political career at my feet which I felt matched my Christian faith and values.

"I remember a moment in the building where the residential selection school to test vocations was held. I found myself walking down the staircase suffused with a sense of peace thinking, if they say 'No, we do not think you have a vocation to the ministry', I would be delighted and I would be free to return to a political vocation with a new sense of motivation and fulfillment. But if they said, 'You are called to the ministry', I would be happy too."

"And thus you were called?"

"Yes."

"And thus the church became your life mission with a strong engagement with politics?"

"Yes, the relationship between religion and politics has been central to my academic career and my public engagement as a civic activist ever since."

In both Briony's and Will's decisions, I see the need to question your life purpose at play. Nothing beats questioning in leading you to a meaningful life. If your life is meaningful, you will be happy.

PART TWO

What is spiritual intelligence?
How can you make it work for you?

I got an excellent explanation of spiritual intelligence from a person with a lifetime of meditation practice. Yogesh Sharda, a teacher and practitioner of Rajyoga meditation based out of Turkey, started to meditate when he was all of nine years old. His parents introduced him to meditation and he took to it naturally, waking up early morning to meditate. So by the time he went to school, he had already been up many hours!

I was tickled to hear that.

"Did your friends express any interest in meditation?" I asked.

"A few seemed intrigued. I would draw charts to explain stuff to them," he said, and shrugged. "I felt fortunate to know what I did."

"You took to meditation very easily," I said, "as though you were made to be a yogi (a meditator). So tell me, Yogesh, what is spiritual intelligence, according to you?"

"Before we get to spiritual intelligence, let's just focus on intelligence to get some context," said Yogesh.

"Okay," I agreed.

"Intelligence can be interpreted in various ways," he continued. "Intelligence is typically associated with knowing."

I nodded.

"But intelligence is not just accumulating information. It is knowing how to appropriately apply that information. I'll run through the types of intelligence to explain.

"The intelligence that we most commonly discuss is IQ. Intelligence quotient. It pertains to rational intelligence, logic, reason and so on."

I nodded.

"When does IQ come in handy?" Yogesh asked.

"You tell me," I said with a smile.

"You need IQ when you're dealing with things, resources. When you are planning something, you need rational intelligence."

"Okay," I said.

"You also have IC, short for intuitive capacity, which is your ability to tap into and listen to your inner wisdom."

"Seriously, Yogesh, does everyone have inner wisdom," I asked.

"Yes. If you're wondering why IC isn't always obvious, it is because to access your IC, you need to quiet the chattering mind. Not everyone can do that. But for those who want to, meditation really helps.

"Then you have EQ. Emotional quotient, symbolizing emotional intelligence. You need EQ when you are dealing with people, to manage your relationships with other people."

"True, emotions usually emerge from interpersonal relationships," I said.

"Relationships can give rise to negative emotions like fear, bitterness and so on. EQ helps us manage those feelings. It helps us improve our relationships. So that is another huge area to work on and explore."

"Yes," I agreed.

"Then you have SQ. Spiritual quotient, symbolizing spiritual intelligence. It relates to your relationship with yourself."

"So you're connecting the word 'spiritual' with the spirit or the energy within," I observed.

"Yes," he said.

"Does that mean that spiritual intelligence helps you be the best person you want to be?" I asked.

"Absolutely," he said. "Consider questions like - how do you feel about yourself? Are you happy with yourself? Do you like yourself? Are you able to maintain a high level of self esteem?

"A spiritually intelligent person would answer 'yes' to those questions. Spiritually intelligent people are a good friend to themselves. They go easy on themselves if they make a mistake. The quality of their self talk doesn't fall. They have a good, healthy self relationship."

"That's very interesting," I said, and then asked Yogesh a question that was nagging me. "How can you tell if someone is spiritually intelligent?"

"Well, I can describe two traits I have seen in people who I consider to have high SQ," said Yogesh. "The first is they own their motivation. Essentially, their motivation is theirs. It belongs to them."

"So they never lose steam," I remarked. "They keep going."

"Yes," he said. "I find most people tend to lose motivation quite easily. They start to do something with huge enthusiasm, huge energy. Then they lose that motivation. Ask them, you had so much motivation to do this, what happened?"

I chuckled but said nothing.

"The commonest answer is 'I got bored'," said Yogesh. "Or, 'I give up'."

"Essentially, they got distracted. They let a situation or someone's comment take away their motivation. But you know what, that means their motivation came from the wrong place. When your motivation is external, it is emotional motivation."

"How true," I said.

"In contrast, spiritual motivation is inner motivation," he continued. "It comes from knowing yourself very well. And so, it lasts not just through your job but through your life. Even if you fail at something you don't lose your motivation, it just doubles your motivation to do better."

"When you say spiritual intelligence comes from knowing yourself very well, what exactly do you mean?"

"You know who you are and you know your purpose," he replied. "Let me explain. If you tell someone 'You are a soul', a lot of people may say 'Yes, I know I am a soul'. But the thing is, to know something doesn't mean anything, as I said at the outset. I know I am a spiritual being. So what? To know is just a piece of information. The important thing is do you accept it."

"Ah," I said.

"Do you accept that this applies to you? That this is not just some general theory floating out there but that you really are a spiritual being? And it doesn't stop there. Okay, you may accept it but can you apply it in life to evolve?"

"Theoretical knowledge alone is no good," I opined.

"Yes, the inner journey is not aimless. It is about reaching my authentic self. Spiritually speaking, movement means my self esteem should become deeper and deeper, my heart should become bigger, which means my capacity to love should increase, my tolerance should become more stable and the energies of anger, fear, sadness, revenge should reduce in my life."

It was a treat to hear Yogesh speak. He spoke with an ease that comes from many years of spiritual practice.

"The French Jesuit priest, philosopher and paleontologist Pierre Teilhard de Chardin very correctly said 'We are not physical beings having a spiritual experience, we are spiritual beings having a physical experience'."

"That's lovely," I said.

"And that is only part of it, the part that has to do with your sense of identity," he smiled. "The other part pertains to your sense of direction and your sense of purpose. Where am I going with my life? And why?"

"So people with high SQ are very focused," I said.

"Yes, and that is why they are successful in what they do," he said. "It isn't as if they don't experience storms but they know how to refocus when the going gets tough."

"How would you recommend that someone acquire such intense focus?" I asked.

"Asking the right questions and reflecting until you get definite answers helps," said Yogesh.

Again, the questioning thread!

"You could ask: if I keep living the way I am living, where is this taking me.

"If I keep using my thoughts, my words and my actions the way I am, where is this going to end up?

"If I keep using my time and my energy the way I currently am, which direction will it take me?

"If I live with the values I currently have, what will be the result?

"The idea is to know why you are on the planet, what you want to do and why you want to do it, so that you don't end up doing stuff just because you see others doing so. There is no need to run with the masses. You need to be clear about the energy driving your life. If you don't know why you are doing what you are doing, then it is possible you may not be doing it for very long. Some people or something will push you in another direction. Something will attract your attention and cause you to drift."

"How true," I said.

"Clarity allows people with high SQ to develop a deep inner sense of contentment, which stays alive even when they pass through adversity, failure or criticism."

"What could be more useful than that," I said. To stay calm amid chaos. My friend Glynis German actually defines spiritual intelligence as being in a state where everything is always fine in my world so I don't react in a negative or positive way.

Glynis works as a wedding celebrant on the island of Majorca. She also hosts a radio show (Just Glynis) and runs a Death Café (if you please) where people come together to discuss, what else, death (truly innovative).

"When there is no spiritual intelligence or maturity at any level, we react about everything going on around us," she said. "So we get sad when we see awful things happening. We get happy when happy things happen to us. There is no intelligence."

"Right," I said. "And how do we move to a stable state?"

"Stability comes from knowing who we are and remembering that," she said.

I loved that Glynis' view reinforced Yogesh's experience. When two spiritually evolved people attest to the usefulness of a perspective, it gets strengthened.

"I'll give you an example. My pet peeve is reacting against bad drivers. As long as I am aware that I am a spirit and the bad driver is a spirit, I'm good. But it isn't easy. I keep forgetting who I am and then lose my cool. I'm hoping that one day before I die I will have reached that plateau where nothing upsets me."

"You can say that again," I said.

How does spiritual intelligence compare with emotional intelligence?

I've travelled to India about thirty times since my first visit in 1991.

I was chatting to a friend and fellow Canadian Judy Johnson, a qualified and successful facilitator and specialist in organizational development, and lest I forget, one of my mentors for this book project, and she told me that she had also been to India about thirty times in the last two decades, "…and that after I swore that I would never visit India in my life," she said.

"That is a rather harsh statement for anyone to make," I remarked. "Where did it come from?"

"I don't know. When I was thirteen, a group of Pakistanis moved into our very white neighborhood in Calgary. It was common for us to hear people use bad language to describe the newcomers," Judy said.

"I couldn't understand the racism towards people of Asian origin. At the time I got hold of two books, a biography of Mahatma Gandhi, and Freedom at Midnight, by the journalists Larry Collins and Dominique Lapierre, which describes events around the Indian independence and partition, and locked myself in my room until I had read the books from cover to cover.

"I didn't understand anything about the politics in the book. But I felt as if I knew the inside of the story that I had just read. Later, after working in the developing world for many years, I declared that I would never visit India. I had the feeling that I never wanted to return to that place."

"That sounds crazy," I said.

Judy nodded.

"Why do you think you felt that way?" I asked.

"Now I understand that the soul had been there [India] before, and for some reason it was resisting going back."

"How did you figure that out?" I asked.

"I think this was a type of spiritual intelligence," Judy said.

I was intrigued. "Tell me more." I said.

"Well, you know how in the spy world or the intelligence world they are always talking about intel or information?"

I nodded.

"Spiritual intelligence is intel or knowledge of the spirit, the life within, which you can feel but not see with your physical senses. Just as emotional intelligence reflects an understanding of emotions. It is kind of like looking at the world through the lens of the spirit, which means you have access to a whole other realm of information than you normally have if you are looking at the world through the physical level, or through the emotional or psychological level."

"That's heavy," I said.

"Let me give you an example," Judy said.

"During my growing years I realized that I was very different from my family. I didn't quite fit in, in the sense that I usually reacted differently than they did to situations."

"Isn't that something that happens fairly commonly?" I said. "Children tend to think differently to their parents, don't they?"

"Yes, although many children tend to emulate their parents. In my case, the difference bothered me. I spent a lot of energy trying to figure out why I was so different," Judy said.

"Emotional intelligence helped me decipher my emotions, my anger, my frustration, based on the immediate triggers, but it didn't help me understand the source of these deeper feelings. The only answer I had was, well, because my parents raised me like this or whatever."

"Wasn't that enough to satisfy you?"

"No, but I didn't know better, until many years later, when I began studying meditation and developed this spiritual intelligence about it. I developed a metaphysical view of the universe and the souls that inhabit it and are journeying through time, and this view gave me a much bigger lens than I ever had before."

"So how did your newfound intel help you?"

"Matters of the spirit are eternal and involve a much bigger picture than say, a geographic view, but it is also very micro in the sense that I can detect what is going on inside me, behind the feeling and behind the thoughts."

Ah, I said. And what did you figure out about yourself?

"I understood that it wasn't as if I came from another genetic pool. I understood that this soul, me, really needed to be raised in the very homogenized, white, middle class neighborhood I grew up in because I needed to be safe. I understood that I, the soul, had a different journey than my family, but in my own journey, that little pit stop was a really good thing for me. It may have been boring. I may not have fit in. I railed against it at the time. But in retrospect I can look at the bigger picture and think this is what the soul needed, a little time out, a totally safe environment to be in, where nothing was challenging or frightening or unsafe."

"Hmm, so, would you say that spiritual intelligence is more useful than to emotional intelligence?"

"I'd say they are both very important. You can look at your own life and you can look at situations and you can understand both with a much bigger perspective. At least, that is what spiritual intelligence has done for me. I couldn't have known what I did about myself with emotional intelligence, but I could know it with my knowledge of the spirit. Seeing the bigger canvas has helped me react very differently to situations."

"Like how," I asked.

"Like I don't have knee-jerk reactions to triggers any more, or rarely do," said Judy. "I think this is really important because we live in an over-reactive world, whether at the level of politicians and countries, or in our individual lives."

That is so true, I thought. When the US and the USSR (then) started to test hydrogen bombs in 1953 the needle of the Doomsday Clock was moved to two minutes before midnight. It has moved back and forth ever since but the fact that it was moved back to that dire position in 2018 suggests we have not done well in moving towards peace on earth. Of course, now the environment is in a mess too. It wasn't in such a bad shape in the fifties.

"People are very quick with an emotional response or opinion nowadays," said Judy. "Then the body follows the emotional reaction. Then we've got war and we've got all kinds of things happening.

For me, it has been a relief to move away from that reactive way of being. I think the world needs that. We need to step back and find out what's really going on with the human spirit.

"We need to calm down. With spiritual intelligence, you see a truth that is much larger than the individual moment. When people speak, you can pick up the truth, you can pick up their vibe which you might have missed if you were not spiritually tuned in. We all need to see the bigger picture."

"By that, do you mean we need to be more holistic in our outlook?"

"Yes, we need to see the impact of our thoughts and actions on the long term. We need to think beyond the present moment."

How can you acquire emotional intelligence and spiritual intelligence?

Having understood what IQ, EQ and SQ are, it is fair to say that the ideal situation is to have all three in adequate measure.

In conversation with Charlie Hogg, director of the Brahma Kumaris, Australia, I found it fascinating to learn how meditation had helped him acquire two of these three kinds of intelligence.

"Charlie, can you tell me what made you feel that you needed spiritual intelligence in the first place?"

"Well, if I think back to when I was in my late teens, I was a pretty average person. I was sensitive. I was okay a lot of the time but I was also very defined by peoples' vision of me. How people saw me influenced how I saw myself a lot."

"How was that?" I asked.

"You know how it is when you are touchy or vulnerable to external impressions? A few words or comments from somebody can put your mind in overdrive, self doubt or worry.

"I might hold a fantastic position, everyone praises me, I run the show, I am an entrepreneur or I am a manager. Yet inside, I feel inadequate."

"Yes, I've been there," I said, recollecting how small I had felt in the company of great souls like Mother Theresa (her sacrifice for humanity just blew me away), Nelson Mandela (I couldn't fathom how he could have spent so many years in jail and not be bitter) and why, even my friend Samuel Kimbriel (how can someone with phenomenal intellectual capacity be so humble, how can a person gain clarity of purpose so young in life, he must be just about thirty).

"Charlie, how old were you when you became aware of all this?"

"I was about twenty. Back then I chose to I wander around South East Asia, India, Africa, living in religious communities. I began to meditate and it was then that I observed how easily I was influenced. I also realized that I had no capacity to stop thoughts of self doubt or worry. I could observe what was happening but I could not stop what was happening."

"That was quite some realization for a twenty year old," I remarked.

"Yes, it was. I realized that even though I had had a very good education which had given me some intellectual ability, IQ, I didn't know who I was or how I functioned."

"And then?" I asked.

"And then I began to see how I had three distinct personalities within myself."

"The first personality was one I call the eye of arrogance or the eye of superiority. It is a personality we create based on our perception of the self as a temporary body with a whole lot of labels. When I identify with that eye of arrogance, I compare myself with others and think I know more, I am right."

"Is that ego?" I asked, squirming to think of myself before I developed any type of spiritual awareness. If I met someone who was poor, I would act like I was smarter or knew more than they did.

"Yes, it is. When I am being deceived by my ego, I feel insulted, disrespected, not valued, excluded and sensitive."

"We've all been there," I said, "realizing that however much intellectual ability is useful it isn't enough to protect me from being deceived by my ego."

"Yes, we have Betty, and I've already described the second personality I identified, which I suffered from a lot, the eye of lack of self respect or the eye of inferiority. This eye also compares but it goes the other way. It thinks others know more. It thinks others don't love me or don't respect me or don't value me. When it merges into my emotions and feelings I feel hopeless, I feel inadequate, I feel unworthy and I feel depressed."

I nodded. I found it fascinating that Charlie could speak of arrogance and inferiority - two emotions I usually see as poles apart - in the same breath, as outcomes of a misplaced understanding of the self.

"Very interesting," I said. "When did you practically start to experience your true self?"

"After travelling through Asia and Africa I visited London where I lived with Hindus, Buddhists, Sikhs, Muslims and Taoists. I didn't just attend lectures. I actually lived in communities. There it became clear to me that the intellect can understand philosophy and concepts but spiritual intelligence transforms theory into an experience. There my meditation grew deeper and I started to convert my belief system into experience."

"So what has acquiring spiritual intelligence done for you?"

"What I found Betty was that the more I became spiritual, the more I was able to understand people, and have mercy and benevolent feelings for people even when they are difficult or rude."

"That's pretty useful," I remarked.

"I also acquired the ability to not judge people based on the temporary labels their body represents but tune into their soul and understand what they are feeling. So in a sense, becoming spiritually intelligence made me more emotionally intelligent."

"What about yourself? How has becoming spiritually intelligent helped you care for yourself?"

"It has helped me care for my mind. If you think of it, don't we live through the mind? Your thoughts, your feelings, your reactions, your memories, your relationships, essentially, all the processing of your existence happens in the mind. We use our mind for everything in life and yet we don't understand how to deal with it and as a result, sometimes, we succumb to chronic negative thinking."

"So are you more level-headed now?"

"Now I understand that the mind is where thoughts originate, and I have learned how to manage my mind, which means, when my thoughts aren't happy thoughts because of what I am going through, I can work with them and bring them back to a happier and even cheerful state," said Charlie.

"What about being touchy?"

"Now I don't give my self-respect away to a person or situation. Also, I relax more. I understand the nature of existence a lot more."

"Do you feel more powerful?"

"If you're thinking of inner power, then the answer is yes."

Here, I'd like to take a moment to share what Pilar said about spiritual intelligence. "Spiritual after intelligence has always led me to think that it is assumed that there is something else, something more powerful that gives strength to intelligence."

I liked that because it is so true. Pure rational intelligence can only get you so far in life. Spirituality opens up doors to your inner world.

Charlie has been practicing Raja Yoga meditation since forty-three years. It was enlightening to learn what a lifetime of spiritual endeavor had done for him.

During our conversation, Charlie remembered the late Anthony Strano, a Raja Yoga meditation teacher who was based in Greece, who I had the good fortune to get to know before he passed in 2014.

Charlie held Anthony up as a rare person with the balance of IQ, EQ and SQ. He had an amazing intellectual capacity, he was very humble, which is the basis of EQ, and hence could engage and connect really well with people, and he had the gift to articulate spirituality and use language to explain the deepest truths in a way that people could connect to.

I endorse this from the bottom of my heart. Anthony was the best spiritual teacher I ever had, starting from the word go.

I first met Anthony at the Oxford Retreat Center of the Brahma Kumaris in 2000. He wanted me to spend the afternoon in silence. Boy, did I resist!

I went into panic mode but he showed no sympathy and just said 'go'.

I (obediently) went into the beautiful English garden and sat very uncomfortably for about an hour.

I was uptight and nervous. And then all of a sudden, I started to enjoy the silence.

Trust Anthony to know how to set me on the spiritual path. Later on in life I got to know that he loved plants very much. When you sat in his living room, the tables in front of you were so full of plants of every shape and size that if Anthony were sitting across from you, you wouldn't see him for all the greenery!

The next time I saw Anthony, we were at a Spanish retreat. He spoke with great clarity. I was so impressed and asked if I could spend some time with him in Athens where he was the coordinator of the Brahma Kumaris center. I felt I could learn a lot from him.

He found me a flat close to the center to stay, so I went.

I arrived in Athens on the Easter weekend. This was in 2014 just months before he left this world. He very kindly arranged a dinner party for me and called all of his contacts in Athens, people who were not practicing Raja Yoga meditation, probably to make me feel at ease. The interactions were great and until today I am in contact with many of that group. Anthony was very gracious, very kind in a quiet way.

When I left Athens I asked him what I could buy him as a present. Guess what his answer was - a plant! I set off to find the most beautiful and rarest plant I could find.

I rate Anthony as the best spiritual teacher I had because of his clarity on all spiritual aspects.

Charlie's take was that Anthony's articulation of deep ideas was so powerful because he spoke from experience. Anthony loved silence. He was really an old saint or sage-styled person who loved to go off to think. And his thinking was in the spiritual intelligence zone, it wasn't just intellectual analysis. He actually experienced what he was thinking and that is why he could articulate it so well.

"And that is what people want, Betty," said Charlie. "People go to seminars and read books by teachers who have phenomenal intellects but they don't really practice much and hence, their writing is mostly theory, a belief system. So despite acquiring information, people find they can't change. They can't transfer it into experience but Anthony was able to transfer wisdom into spiritual experience and then articulate it for others."

"Anthony was full of love and so compassionate," I remarked to Charlie. "I think that was why he was very patient with me and would explain things over and over again until I got the point. And he was so lost in his love for God."

I remember I once asked Anthony, "Who do you really care about? What do you really care about?"

He said, "I just care about God".

And he said it in a really matter of fact way.

"When you have such a deep relationship with God you can be genuinely compassionate and detached and loving and benevolent," Charlie explained. "Being lost in love for God pulls you beyond human likes, dislikes and all the human stuff in relationships, so you can be genuinely detached and maintain your situation. For me there can be no higher or purer life than one where you are in love with God and your life, your behavior, your face and your attitude pulls others in that direction too. And Anthony was such a person."

So much can come from balancing your IQ, EQ and SQ.

PART THREE

What do you know of God?

What do I know of God?

As a child, I was taught that someone up there was looking after me. He was protecting me and keeping me away from evil. It was very natural and it made sense... until I lost a baby to a heart disorder in the early years of my marriage. I blamed God for her death. He was supposed to have been looking out for me - and He hadn't (I thought). I felt let down. I was angry. People around told me that God had a plan and that made me angrier still.

Unable to come to terms with the grief, in the ensuing years, I engaged with rabbis (my husband was Jewish and I had converted before we were married), hoping to understand why Terri had gone so young. I never did get a satisfactory answer. Gradually, I developed an aversion to God. I wasn't comfortable talking about Him let alone to Him.

While researching this book, I found it interesting to learn that others had turned away from God too, for reasons of their own.

"A lot of people with western mindsets have rejected religion for a lot of good reasons, I did myself too," said Charlie. "When I was confirmed in church, I got the impression that God is an authoritarian, punishing, judgmental kind of guy, certainly not someone I wanted to know as an eleven or twelve year old. I couldn't relate to that sort of God.

"Today I also understand that one of the big put-offs of a religious relationship with God is it is an indirect relationship. You don't really feel His presence, just the priests' presence."

What comes through from Charlie's statement is that our impressions of God are often built by men of God, by the keepers of religions. I am purposely not including women here because until recently, priests were typically men.

I know my impression of God after Terri died was influenced by the rabbis I engaged with. And they were of no help, as I said.

Charlie had pretty much the same opinion.

"Often when I talk about God I say the religions are like advertising agencies that have done a bad job on the God account," said Charlie.

*

Somewhere around the turn of the century I learned acceptance. I learned how to be comfortable with the fact that Terri had been a part of my life and she would always be in my heart. I learned not to bury sorrow but to feel joy in the joy I once had.

What helped?

I cannot pinpoint one thing. Exposure to life, exposure to the world, exposure to sadness helps you realize that life isn't perfect, or to put it philosophically, life is perfect in all its imperfections. Hearing from great men and women inspired me to think about life. Here, I must mention my favorite poet-singer, the late Leonard Cohen. "Forget your perfect offering, there is a crack in everything, that's how the light gets in," words from Cohen's Anthem, a song sung in 1992 that became an anthem of hope especially in hard times. I learned to accept the bad in life and find the silver lining in every adversity.

Marilyn Mazzotta, a friend of mine (more on her later) says, "Bad things happen to good people because it is the good people who show others how to get through bad things."

My association with the Brahma Kumaris starting in 1990 also helped. It exposed me to many workshops on God. About five years ago during one such workshop on God led by Jayanti I finally said the G-word. She looked at me and said, "It only took thirty years."

It has taken me a lifetime to accept God as a benevolent, non- judgmental higher power, without expecting Him to work in a certain way, without feeling betrayed when things don't turn out as I expect. But loving God has always come naturally to one of my interviewees, Gopi. This book is all Gopi's fault, as I've explained in the preface!

Gopi learned to meditate at the age of eight. When she was a child, she said, she lived with spiritual intelligence very easily. "I had a very natural relationship with God and the world. I think the purity of a young child makes it easy to access God."

Gopi said maintaining a relationship with God takes a bit more effort as you grow because you face all sorts of challenges.

"When you face challenges, you can't live unconsciously with knowledge, you need to apply your mind to situations and figure things out," she said.

Gopi's first big test came at the age of fourteen. Her siblings, her grandfather and she had just moved to England from Africa. Her parents were still in Africa. It was a challenging time because she was starting a new education system but more than that because her grandfather had terminal lung cancer and she opted to be his main caregiver.

"I would make his food, put his medication out, go to university and come back and make sure he was fed and go back and forth to college," she said. "I nursed my grandfather for about six months. When he was close to passing away he went through a patch when he suddenly got better and we all thought he was going to improve. And then he passed away all of a sudden and no one was at the hospital. His good days were his last bloom, as they say. I know that now but I didn't know that then."

"You were still very young," I remarked. "His passing must have hit you hard?"

"My first reaction to the sudden turn of events was 'Okay fine, it happens'. It was the classical naive reaction of a teenager."

I waited to hear what she said next.

"Then they brought his body home, as is the custom. That was when the emotional impact of the loss hit me hard because I had invested a lot of energy in him. Crikey, I thought. What if that was me tomorrow? Would there be anything that I would regret not having done?"

"Ah!" I said.

"Seriously, Betty, my grandfather's passing away was a wake-up call to live more consciously with the knowledge that was a part of me. It was a wake-up call to live more consciously. My relationship with God has only grown stronger as I have applied myself to meditation and to deepening my connection with Him."

*

I would like to call out two of my interviewees, Marta Matarin and Samuel, whose love for God seems to be intrinsic to their being. Their love for God is so natural that they have never experienced any struggle in connecting with Him.

Marta, a lovely lady in her forties, has been coordinating the teaching center of the Brahma Kumaris in Barcelona for seventeen years. Like Charlie, Marta comes from a Christian background where God is seen as the one who would punish you.

"Looking back, considering how we were brought up, it doesn't surprise me that many people just don't want to know God," she said.

Still, she told me that from a young age, she believed that God would always love her no matter what.

"As a little child I couldn't imagine a God who did not love humanity... then it wouldn't be God," she said simply.

With that sort of a bond with God, it didn't surprise me to next hear Marta say, "You can't reach a higher level of spiritual intelligence without letting God be a part of your life... You must accept God as a higher energy. But not everyone is ready for that because acknowledging God would necessitate one to change... and many people are not ready to change."

"There was never a time when I didn't know God," said Samuel.

"When I think about my earliest consciousness, there is no way for me to point to myself and say this is me without that awareness. I knew God and I knew that He loves me. Those things were basic to me from the moment I opened my eyes."

"Where do you think that knowing came from?" I asked.

"Maybe it came from my mothers' prayers? That's possible. But it wasn't something I had because they implanted it in me. It wasn't something new that came to me. Awareness of God is just me."

Samuel was of the opinion that in general, people in the West are less aware of God than people in the developing world. He narrated a story of a Black African who was around a White European who was always cursing God.

"And she (the Black African) asked, 'I don't understand how he can do that? Isn't he afraid that God would strike him down?'"

"And she was told, 'Well, he doesn't believe in God.'"

"She couldn't understand that. For her, God is not something to guess about, it is completely obvious that He exists."

*

What happens when you know God as He is? Your vision becomes one of universal brotherhood (or sisterhood). You genuinely feel for the world and want the good of all.

Truly knowing God is an equalizer, I feel.

Marta told me she was shocked when as a child she would go to church and they would say let's pray for the Christians. "Inside myself I would say, and for the Muslims and for the Buddhists... I knew there were other types of people. I believed in a holistic concept of community. I believed that God was God for everyone. I couldn't understand how you can pray only for people of one religion and not for the others."

That made a lot of sense to me. Today, I associate spirituality with God, to the extent that He is the source of all the good we want for the world. That implies greater acceptance, reflecting values in life, living honestly.

If someone were to say to me, 'I believe in God', but then that person, were to display a divisive vision, I would say such belief is of no use.

"God is all in all. This is at the heart of Christianity. There is a single deity. And He profoundly loves us," said Samuel.

All of us...

Don't tell God what to do

In the last chapter, I wrote about knowing God, about building a relationship with God. I mentioned in passing that it has taken me a lifetime (well, almost) to learn not to expect Him to work in a certain way.

I really do find it fascinating how we (including me, until a few years ago) tend to think that knowing God - and building a relationship with Him - entitles us to ask Him for stuff.

That job. That raise. That niggling health problem. That relationship. Winning the lottery. Whatever. Typically, material things.

It doesn't work that way.

When you build a relationship with God, you become entitled to experience any virtue - love, peace, compassion and so on. You name it, you can experience it. That is, provided that you invest in the relationship, and by that, I mean, provided that you connect with Him and keep the connection live.

You want to experience love. It's yours - not for the asking but for knowing God because He is an ocean of love.

You want to experience peace. It's yours - again, not for the asking but for knowing God because He is an ocean of peace.

In the last couple of decades, my practice of communion with God has evolved from saying a prayer, a routine I picked up in church, to meditation, which involves sitting quietly to collect my thoughts, trying to still the mind and focus on Him.

I find meditation a pleasurable experience. It is when some great ideas have popped into my head. It is also when I ask of Him...

I think of God as my protector and so yes, sometimes I ask Him for help to sort out something. However, I don't ask Him to fix anything, I ask Him to show me the way.

Understanding how God works can bring peace to your life besides help you navigate your way through the chaos that life often turns out to be.

My friend Savi Balladin came about this realization - "You don't tell God what to do," to quote her - at a very critical time in her life - when she had almost lost her daughter to an unknown viral disease.

Savi was in those days - as she is now - the coordinator of the Toronto chapter of the Brahma Kumaris, a meditation center I visit whenever I am in town. It's quite a happening place on the weekends - up to 250 practitioners can congregate for group meditation. Savi and her colleague run the place very efficiently. I enjoy these sessions plus of course I enjoy spending time with Savi, someone who I care for and trust.

To get back to her story -

"My daughter fell very sick when she was about twenty-three years old, when she was doing her Masters," said Savi.

"We admitted her to hospital - she was in intensive care - but the doctors struggled to identify her disease," she said. "They couldn't figure out what virus was causing her sickness. Gradually her condition worsened. At one point we thought we would lose her, at least, that is what the doctors told us to prepare for.

"I called a senior sister associated with the Brahma Kumaris in

London and said ,'I think she will go, that is what the doctors are saying'. She said 'Play Baba's (implying God's, baba means father in Hindi) music and let Baba (implying God) take care of her'.

"She also told me that she would ask a senior Raja Yoga teacher based out of New York to fly to Toronto."

"That was kind," I remarked. I understood that the senior sister in London had been referring to God when she used the word Baba and that Baba's music was tunes and songs that the Brahma Kumaris use during meditation.

"I thought God was sending someone to share my physical suffering," Savi said. "I was in a bad state by then. I found it hard to see my daughter, to see what was going on in the intensive care. By then, the doctors had given up on her; they had told us that she could go any time. I felt better for being outside. So I said I would receive the sister at the airport.

"When she arrived, I was in the process of arranging our next steps if and when she left the body. I escorted her to the hospital but I didn't enter the room where my daughter lay. She entered alone."

I nodded. I was all ears, fully engrossed in the story.

"After some time the sister came out and said 'She still has life in her. The soul is still there. I'll stay with her'.

"I told her that I would leave after some time but my sister would come soon to relieve me. She went back into the room and sat with my daughter and started talking to her.

"I waited outside for some time. I remember standing at a large hospital window saying 'God, just take her. I'll be okay. Let her go. Let her get a new body. Let her enter a new womb.'"

Hearing Savi speak, I was reminded of my own time with my daughter Terri, how at one point it had made sense to tell the doctors to pull the plug. It was so hard to do despite being the right thing to do. Suddenly my reminiscing ended and I heard Savi continue.

"All this time the sister was talking to my daughter in the room. Suddenly she responded and from that moment onwards she got better and better."

"Wow," I said. "And is she okay now?"

"She lost the function of one lung to that virus but she has been managing well ever since. She takes good care of herself."

Savi looked thoughtful.

"After everything was said and done my realization was 'you don't tell God what to do'."

I chuckled and nodded. "I ask Him to show me the way," I said. "Of course that involves listening to Him and being aware of signs because He does communicate."

"Before that incident," Savi said, "I used to complain to God every day, and tell Him what to do to make this situation better and that situation better. I don't think that phase of my life was wrong, honestly, the chit chat helped me to develop a relationship with Him."

"That's a very positive outlook," I said.

"Sure," she said. "It was only after my daughter's incident that I surrendered to God. I learned how to leave everything to Him. I realized that you don't tell Him what to do even if you feel close to Him. To the contrary, because you are close to Him, leaving everything to Him seems right."

"So, do you think He knows what to do?"

"I think things happen the way they are meant to. I believe that the world is a stage and that we are all playing our designated roles in this global drama. I believe that He knows what we're going through but He doesn't interfere."

"So, truly, I said, "there's no point telling Him what to do."

We both smiled.

How can knowing God change your life?

In the last couple of chapters I have explored what it means to know God. I described my wavering relationship with God. I felt close to Him in my childhood. I drifted away from Him when I couldn't accept the curveballs life threw at me. Eventually, I became aware that I have always been under His canopy. I shared a couple of examples of people who have been in love with God, if I may put it that way, from a young age. Marta and Sam have never drifted away no matter what.

In this chapter I would like to explore what finding God - or being found by Him - has meant to a woman whose life got off to a wrong start and who has faced a lot of hardship along the way.

I befriended Nancy Stewart on one of my many visits to Mount Abu. She moved into the room next to mine with a helper, piles of food, piles of equipment, and promptly proceeded to take over the place. A few days later she was playing some videos on her iPad and the sound was too loud for comfort. I lost it with her. The upshot of the exchange was we became friends.

To understand what finding God and fulfillment has meant to Nancy, you need to know where she came from. So, over to her for her life story -

"I was born in 1937. I was the third child of a family that farmed a large tract of land (about 1,500 acres) in Scotland. My parents were hard working, privileged people."

"When I was a couple of months old, I developed eczema. I was sent to live near the ocean with a maid. There, I underwent treatment for my skin condition. It involved being painted with coal tar. I used to be tied to a crucifix to prevent me from scratching."

I was horrified to hear about the treatment given to an infant. I thought 'how cruel' but I all I said was, "Crucifix, Nancy? Is that what you said?"

It sounded unbelievable.

Nodding, Nancy said, "It must have affected my life".

Of course it must have. As I said, you need to know where Nancy came from to understand what fulfillment has meant to her.

"How long did that treatment last?" I asked.

"About two years."

Nancy continued her story.

"My younger sister was born in 1940. She was a war baby. I knew nothing about that. I went to a private school for about eleven years, and was then sent to boarding school where the teachers' ideology was don't spare the rod for the child."

"Oh dear," I said.

"Oh yes! We were taught to keep a stiff upper lip."

"So you were never treated like children?"

"Our teachers believed that children should be seen and not heard."

It got worse.

"My parents never visited on visiting Sundays and that left me feeling quite rejected and depressed. At the age of fifteen, I ran away taking five girls with me."

"Goodness Nancy!"

"I know. Terrible! I got expelled. Then I was sent to finishing school in Switzerland for a few years. When I came home, my father said he didn't feel like spending any more money on my education and it was time I looked after myself. So I started to train as a registered nurse in a hospital. It was tough but I felt happy for the first time in my life. I felt needed and fulfilled."

I nodded. To hear her use the word 'fulfilled', I realized what the escape would have meant to her.

"After four years I trained in midwifery in St Andrews and stayed there until 1960 when I got married after a five-year courtship."

The marriage turned out to be abusive.

I waited patiently for her to continue.

"I waited until my father died to get divorced," she said.

"Why, Nancy? Why did you subject yourself to more misery?"

"Because getting divorced wasn't something one did in Scotland in 1960."

"Ah!" I said. I understood that only too well. When I got divorced in the eighties, I had faced plenty of people who didn't want to know me, a divorcee. Or if they knew me, they started to ignore me. Nancy went through the same.

"I didn't want my dad to know my marriage was a failure. So I waited. After I got divorced, people cut me off. I started to look everywhere for a job. I found employment as a matron of a private nursing home. It was at the seaside and the place had an excellent school nearby, which was important to me. I wanted my daughters to study well. I worked hard. I did well. Eventually, I opened my own nursing home."

Nancy did remarkably well professionally. She served lords and ladies and all sorts of well placed people. She worked until the age of sixty when she sold off her assets. By that time her daughters were married. She had remained frugal in her ways and ended up saving a lot.

What did you do after that?

"I travelled to Bangkok with a backpack looking for spirituality. I didn't find God but I visited a lot of beach huts and met all sorts of people and did all sorts of silly things."

I chuckled at the thought of Nancy backpacking her way through South-East Asia.

"The next year I travelled around southern Europe in a camper van. My children and grandchildren joined me and we had some great holidays. The years flew by. In 2005, one of my daughters called me one day and said her family was travelling to Mauritius for Christmas for three weeks. She asked me if I would like to join them.

"It sounded like fun. So I booked myself a place to stay as I didn't want to be on top of them. We had a great time. Then they left and I thought what am I going to do now?"

"And what did you do," I prompted.

"I came upon a signboard of a Raja Yoga meditation center. I resisted going in but I felt as if a lasso had been thrown over me, I felt so drawn to visit."

I sighed. I remembered the numerous times I had thought up excuses to travel to Mount Abu. For a long time I didn't understand the pull to that place that I loved and hated at the same time. I would find excuses to visit - to work at the hospital, to meet old friends and so on but never would I admit the reason was God.

"Betty," said Nancy. "I found God at the age of sixty-eight. I mean I always knew about the spirit and the Supreme spirit. I knew about that from the Bible. But this was different. When I learned how to meditate, I felt I was truly connecting with God. And the Brahma Kumaris' interpretation of time helped me make sense of the world."

I nodded.

"I felt happy, so happy that I couldn't contain my happiness. I felt like sharing my newfound knowledge with every tourist I met."

"Goodness, and did you?" I asked.

"I did. On the beaches of Mauritius, I would speak to every foreigner I met!" recounted Nancy with obvious glee.

"Wow!"

"Over the next five months I experienced great inner-change, which reflected in my lifestyle. I quit smoking in one day and that says a lot because I was addicted to Slim Panatellas (cigars). I gave up wine and liqueurs. I became a vegetarian. I eliminated garlic and onions from my diet. The best part was all these changes happened so easily. It was like I lost my desire for those indulgences because I had found something much better."

"That is amazing," I said.

"I bought so many books to read," Nancy continued. "When I was returning I wanted to take them all with me. I got to the airport and the man who was checking me in said 'You're twenty kilos overweight' and he asked me to pay excess baggage. I don't know what came over me but I said 'That is God's bag and God does not pay'."

I laughed and laughed.

"I was so intoxicated with God's love, Betty."

I sobered up. I nodded. "Yes, and that is what I find beautiful," I said. "So did you eventually pay for the excess luggage?"

"No way," said Nancy. "The man went to his boss who asked him to let me through. You know, God doesn't pay."

I chuckled. Nancy continued her story.

"Some time later I was introduced to Dadi Janki (the present head of the Brahma Kumaris) and I said to her 'I have fallen in love with God'.

"'We will not have an engagement,' she said. 'We will get married straight away!'"

I burst into peals of laughter.

"Dadi promptly slipped a gold ring on my finger, and she advised me to spend half of my time in London and half in India, in Mount Abu, which I have done even though Indian food has nearly killed me!"

I smiled to hear that since I find Indian food hard to digest as well.

So if you had to summarize how your life changed after learning how to meditate, Nancy, what would you say? I asked.

"Before I met Baba (implying God, baba means father in Hindi), I felt empty. I now feel full."

For me, that is the punch line of Nancy's interview.

While Nancy's life circumstances were fairly extreme, we live in a world where hardly anyone escapes seeing sorrow from close quarters. Many of us carry that sorrow to the grave. I love Nancy's story because it shows you can let it go and feel fulfilled. To know God is to open yourself to love.

God. Religion. Spirituality.
Can you do without any?

Religion is supposed to be about God. Religion is also about faith. Faith implies an absence of questioning, something I am incapable of.

In a previous chapter, I explored why a few people I know (and me) drifted away from God - and why I came back to His fold. When I didn't get the answers I was looking for from men of God, I drifted away from both religion and God.

When I interviewed Yogesh, he recollected an interesting comment by Gandhi. "Those who believe religion and politics aren't connected don't understand either."

I have come to believe that both politicians and religious leaders don't like being questioned. They both seek followers. And yes, a lot of very successful politicians (like Donald Trump) use religion all the time. They know the worth of rallying a whole section of the population.

Talking to the National Post earlier this year, Margaret Trudeau (one of my interviewees who I'll introduce in greater detail ahead, here let me just say that she is nowadays best known for being the mother of the current Canadian prime minister, Justin Trudeau, however, she was also wife of the former prime minister of Canada Pierre Elliott Trudeau) said her faith in the great religions had waned after an audience she and Pierre had with the Pope in Rome resulted not in a spiritual discussion but in a literal pat on the head and his observation that she was 'blessed among women' for bearing children. Ditto an interaction with the Dalai Lama in which, she says, he called her 'the mother of the world'.

"Two religious world leaders talking about me as an important mother figure. It was a little grandiose," she said.

Mathilde Sergeant, a meditation practitioner and a qualified nurse with a lifetime of nursing experience who I have known almost since she relocated permanently to India from the Netherlands in the mid-nineties, told me she drifted away from religion when as a young, eager missionary nurse in Africa many years ago she saw the cracks in Christianity.

"I became a missionary to follow God's order to bring peace on earth. I had always thought that I would serve in Africa. I studied nursing for that purpose," she said. "But my dream shattered soon after I got there. I saw the local people happily praying to their God dressed in their beautiful colorful attire, dancing even, as part of their worship. I loved that, I even joined a group and danced with them. And then, we were asked to encourage them to convert. We made a Protestant church, a Catholic church in the villages. It didn't seem right. This cannot be, I said. This is not what God wants.

"Then one day a few patients died because of the carelessness of a student nurse. I found the patients dead in their beds. So I said to the one who was responsible, I cannot trust you. You must go home. You must be retrained. As a result of that we were without nurses. All the nurses left because I had sent home the one careless nurse."

I should mention here that Mathilde is a very good nurse, very caring, sincere and conscientious. Back to her story -

"I went alone into the village. I found the people dancing around the dead body. What am I seeing? I thought. They said we are dancing because he died. We also dance when someone is born.

"It was a revelation to see how being born and dying was so integrated in their lives. That was a very big lesson for me. God gives and God takes. We always said this in church and there I saw that in practice. I was very impressed.

"I could no longer align myself to the missionary way of thinking. I couldn't believe that my religion was superior to theirs, my God was the true God. I still loved God but I moved away from organized religion."

Mathilde instead adopted spirituality. Essentially, she held on to God but chucked religion.

Decades after developing anger towards God, I made my peace with Him but continued to stay away from religion.

In the world I grew up in, God and religion went hand in hand. Today, the numbers of people who believe in God but who have shunned practices rooted in blind faith suggest that it needn't be so.

A long-time friend, Prue Chambers, who is a long-serving Anglican minister, made an interesting comment when I interviewed her for this book.

"Religion is something that is met in life and affects your attitude to life, your mental reasoning and social behavior," she said. "Spirituality reflects what you have come to believe and the way you reflect your belief in your lifestyle."

As I see it, what we come to believe is born of our rational thinking mind whereas religion is all about faith.

"Spirituality may well be part of a religious experience but you can have spirituality without a religious practice," affirmed Jenny Kartupelis, a good friend based in Cambridge, UK, who has worked for years for the World Congress of Faiths as the strategy and development officer.

I regarded Jenny's words highly because of her background. Jenny was previously the director (and a co-founder) of the East of England Faiths Council for over a decade, an organization working with the local and national government to promote faith in society and interfaith in the region. In 2010, Jenny was awarded the MBE (member of the Most Excellent Order of the British Empire, a British order of chivalry) for her services to interfaith.

But this chapter is not about bashing religion. It is to urge my reader to question what religion is doing for you. I have friends who have used religion as a base to connect with God and evolve.

Judy Buddle, a former neighbor when my children were young, who was a huge support when my daughter Terri was dying, is a staunch Roman Catholic. For her, the Bible is the last word on God.

So, she accepts that, "God was and always will be. He has not changed nor ever will. He is the creator of the universe, and the creator of all things. He is omnipresent, ever loving, merciful, all forgiving. His greatest creation is humankind. We live because He loves us. We are eternally loved by God, eternal meaning during our few years on earth but more importantly when we finish our few years here, we will die, but our souls live on eternally with him in Heaven. God is the Trinity, Father, Son and Holy Spirit, and God the

Father sent his son Jesus Christ to take on a human life to teach us visually and through His miracles on earth, that God is all powerful and all loving…"

Judy also accepts the admonishment in the Bible against shunning God. In conversation with me, she said, "Those who chose to ignore him or completely reject Him will not be given the opportunity to spend eternity with Him."

When I questioned her on blind faith, she agreed that her beliefs are based on faith, but she said faith is essential because our understanding is too meager to comprehend these mysteries.

In conversation with Glynis about the appalling state of our world, when I asked her why she thought we had got to this state, she said, "I think it is because we have moved away from God, and by that, I mean a religiosity that gives us an awareness of something bigger than us."

I was intrigued. "Tell me more," I said.

"Well, growing up in the sixties and seventies, I grew up in a religious setting, which was pretty normal in those days. However, since the nineties when education and layers of society and the larger shift to secularism took out any religious reference, we took out any awareness of something bigger than us.

"In rejecting God, we rejected all of the things that gave society some structure, and brought us order. We lost our way, our common sense and our values. We reduced the world to a very selfish space."

Indeed, we have.

Jenny made the point of how people living in countries that have seen an influx of refugees have turned against the homeless.

"People find it hard to welcome refugees," she said. "They tend to see them as a mass of people creating a mass of problems. Instead of as individuals who have only one life to be lived, with a need for physical comforts such as food and shelter but also with a need to experience love and joy."

Jenny recollected the Hindu greeting, Namaste, which translates to, 'the spirit within me salutes the spirit in you'. "To me," she said, "that means I see you as another human being without the trappings attached to either of us. I see you as a person with the same sorrows and joys I feel."

I nodded.

I thought of my friend Judy. She had ten children, many adopted from different countries. Clearly, she had used faith to cross the barrier of ethnicity.

"Do you think religion can help us cross the barriers of ethnicity, culture, age and so on, and see others as human beings devoid of those labels," I asked Jenny.

"If you were aware of yourself and had experienced God's love, you would see all people as individuals," said Jenny. "The thing is, professing to have a faith and following its practices doesn't necessarily improve your spiritual life."

"Are you saying that being religious then doesn't necessarily make us better human beings?"

"It should in theory but in practice it often does not," she agreed.

My friend Upkar back in Canada expressed the thought that humanity has gotten lost, in the sense that we have confused religious ideology with spiritual principles.

"Instead of focusing on the spiritual principles of universality and commonality, we started to say if you come from a different sect than mine, or follow a practice that is different to what I practice, you are therefore disconnected from me and mine," he said. "The more points of separation in religious practices, the further it moves away from the universal values and spirituality that it was intended to embody."

"Are you saying that religion and spirituality have different aims?"

"I believe we started out from an ideology of spiritual principles and universality and believing that all people are one, but have reached a point where religion draws divisive lines. Today people have the feeling that you will go to hell if you don't adopt so and so practice or ritual or custom or whatever. However, I believe that if we were to dissect religious practices and go to the fundamental tenets of most religions we will find way more commonality than differences. It is in the interpretation and application of those principles to religious practices that we become differentiated and start to draw distinctions that were not intended or meant to exist."

"So is religion useful at all?" I prodded.

"Faith can have an enormous good value and influence in peoples' lives and for many people it is the way to express their spirituality," said Jenny.

"So how would you suggest people evaluate if their faith is having a good influence on them?" I asked.

"Question if your religious practice is helping you see meaning in your life and meaning in the life of others," said Jenny.

PART FOUR

What do you know of the world?

If it were not for my travelling lifestyle and interest in current global events, I wouldn't really know what is going on in the world. Being aware of what is happening is important to me. To my mind, it is the difference between living in a box and living in contact with the greater world.

I find living in isolation very limiting. I think it hampers self development and restricts your life choices. Let me narrate you an anecdote that I think elucidates this aspect. I heard this from Devindree Pillay, a thoughtful woman from Durban, South Africa, a qualified occupational therapist with her own business.

Psychology was one of Devindree's majors in college during the mid nineties. One of those courses introduced the students to the concept of intelligence and gave them an example to bring out its meaning.

"We were told that intelligence is the ability to survive in any environment no matter where you are," she said. "We were given the example of natives of the Amazon jungle. They are known for being strong and hardy with the ability to walk miles barefoot in a harsh tropical climate.

"Someone conducted an experiment. They took some Amazonian natives to a modern city and found that they were unable to adapt to the new conditions. Essentially, they couldn't survive in a concrete jungle. It was explained that the type of intelligence you develop is based on the environment you live in."

"I love that," I said. It emphasizes my belief that exposure can be very helpful in developing the self. "Did the example make sense to you at the time," I asked.

"It's interesting because I heard that story at a time when I wasn't really aware of current events in South Africa let alone the rest of the world," continued Devindree.

"You must have been very sheltered?"

"I think was very naive. But I thank my teachers for helping to expand my horizon. When I was a teenager South Africa was transitioning from apartheid to democracy. A lot of my teachers were former activists and they looked upon our lessons as opportunities to make us aware of the situation in South Africa. They didn't want to introduce us to party politics but generally apprise us of the crisis that humanity is facing."

"Did you find they were bitter about what they had to go through?"

"No, I found they were passionate about humanity. They certainly helped make me more aware of the need for justice. Equal opportunities became very important for me as did honoring the dignity of every individual. Their sharing also made me aware of the need to be more benevolent and serve the world."

I liked that.

"I remember my English teacher had prescribed a list of novels she wanted us to read. None of those were the conventional classics. They were about subjects like female trafficking, child labor and female circumcision."

I nodded. "How did reading those novels help you?" I asked.

"Those titles opened my ears, eyes, heart and mind, and it was so important for me because my only exposure to life until then was what I had seen on TV and in the movies. After school I studied occupational therapy where again the focus was to understand a person from a social point of view, taking the whole person into consideration and appreciating where individuals come from and where they are heading," continued Devindree.

"And did that further your development?"

"Yes, all of that learning helped develop me spiritually, and of course my exposure to the Brahma Kumaris and Raja Yoga meditation practice during my late teens was a dominant influence."

"How has becoming aware of the state of humanity impacted your life choices?"

"Awareness has helped me understand that the world is in transition. Change is the way of life but I feel the transition we are seeing now is somewhat deeper. I have no idea how long it will take or what form it will take but I see myself as playing a tiny role in helping further this change for the better, to a new earth. I want to be used for humanity in the best way possible."

"Would you say you feel responsible for the world?"

"Awareness has made me feel responsible but it isn't only about a duty. It is a pleasure to contribute to world transformation," she said.

I liked that. I felt a sense of seriousness but no heaviness in her sharing. She giggled at the right places and was breezy about stuff.

Devindree's path to awareness suggests that it helps to stay abreast of what's happening around you.

The idea of an individual contributing to world transformation may seem far-fetched but it isn't really.

Be the change that you wish to see in the world. Remember those famous words of Gandhi? I have many friends, indeed, many interviewees for this book, who have made big time changes to their life to contribute to world transformation.

"There must be a natural expression of our beliefs in my daily life," said Devindree. "You can't only have good intentions."

I couldn't agree more.

Another woman I interviewed, Seeta, a Mauritian settled in Rwanda since 2007, a meditation teacher who commands great respect in the community she lives in, outlined how being aware can impact day to day living.

"Those who are unaware live in the limited realm. Those who are aware live in the unlimited realm.

"Those who are unaware focus on their own life. They focus on temporary pleasures.

"The aware see their life as an opportunity to serve the world, and their body as an instrument for that purpose. They focus on furthering non-violence and brotherhood, and on protecting the environment."

I got to know Seeta when I visited Kigali, in Rwanda, to see the Genocide Museum. I found her the epitome of humility and the perfect host. When she ushered me in to the center, she promptly informed me that the hot water tank had broken. I didn't know what to say. I didn't want to embarrass her in any way.

She went to great lengths to see that I slept comfortably, even stepping out on the balcony to tell her neighbors she had a special guest so to keep quiet. Africa is not a quiet place by any standards.

The next morning I woke up to find that she had heated up water for me. I was very humbled.

Seeta arranged for me to see the Genocide Museum and took me to see the Parliament. The fact that the politicians stood up when she walked in said a lot about their respect for her.

"Seeta, do you think your lifestyle choices have actually made an impact on the world around you?"

"I am peaceful even when the world around me is in chaos. Isn't that a wonder?" she said.

Facing the terrorists, murderers and rapists among us

One Monday afternoon in April 2018, a man in his twenties used a rental van to mow down pedestrians in Toronto.

An observer described the scene as, "From a war zone. There were garbage cans everywhere, broken bus shelters and mailboxes on the ground."

The carnage spread over a couple of kilometers down a busy stretch of road in North York, an area I am familiar with.

Ten people reportedly died, fourteen were injured.

I knew one of those who died. A woman in her fifties, who used to volunteer for me many years ago.

A reporter with the Toronto Star interviewed me on the event. She asked me if I was angry.

I said, "No, I feel empathy."

The reporter got angry with me.

She wanted me to express anger. I think people in general find it easier to face the murderers, the terrorists and the rapists among us with anger. Anger allows them to lump aggressors in a category separate to the rest of us 'civilized' ones, and shun them.

The thing is, expressing anger and locking away perpetrators doesn't help in any way. It doesn't trigger reform. Nor does it help prevent future attacks.

So, what helps?

"Hate the sin, not the sinner," said Jayanti. "Murderers need a huge amount of support and love instead of prison and a sentence. Slamming the door in their face isn't helpful at all. It is very important to reach out and connect even though that isn't easy."

In conversation with Marta, she remembered Jayanti giving her precisely the same advice many years ago when she was launching a meditation program for prisoners. She had asked Jayanti for advice on how to engage with her pupils (a medley of convicts).

"Sister Jayanti asked me if I can separate the person from what the person does?" said Marta.

"So practically, would that mean seeing the energy apart from what the energy does?" I asked.

"Yes. It means just look at the person, at the pure soul. Don't think about why the person is in prison. Actually, I never ask why the person is in prison," she said.

"How has this helped you as a teacher of meditation? How does it impact how you speak to a prisoner?" I asked.

"I don't get affected by the background of a person even if I get to know it. Let me share an example…

"One late evening, during a session in the prison, I said to one person who was part of my group, 'It is time to go.' You see we were not allowed to spend the night in the prison. We had to leave and return the next morning for service.

"I knew the man I was speaking to as a psychologist. I thought he was a professional who was there for service as I was. He turned to me and said 'I stay here'. That was when I realized that I was mistaken. He was an inmate. I couldn't believe it. He was such a normal seeming person. 'Okay, okay,' I said. 'See you tomorrow'.

"The next morning I returned at 7.30 am for morning meditation. The man came up to me and said 'Can I say something?' I nodded.

"'I killed my wife. I cannot see myself as having done that. Something happened and you know, when you get angry and angrier and still angrier, there reaches a point when you cannot control yourself. And when you cross that barrier, you can do anything because you have lost total control of yourself. Now I look back and feel so terrible about what I did but I did it'."

"That must have been quite some conversation," I remarked.

"I appreciated the man for being honest," said Marta. "It was good that he was acknowledging his mistake. Acknowledgment is the first step to right a wrong. Later I came to know that many inmates would never admit what they did."

"So you were not affected at all by his confession?" I asked.

"No," said Marta. "I separated the action - the murder - from the murderer."

What Marta said next was beautiful and so relevant.

"If I kept seeing him as the one who killed his wife, I would not be able to help him overcome anger. For me this relates to spiritual intelligence. Spiritual intelligence is not only about the self. It is also about helping another person overcome their issues."

I had a question. "So it isn't as if you are reducing the intensity of the crime in separating the person from the deed?"

"No, of course I am not," said Marta. "What he did was wrong. I accept that. He needed to serve a prison sentence for the murder. What has to be done has to be done."

I turned to Eric Le Reste for my next question. Eric is a media person based out of Montreal. He makes documentaries for the Canadian Broadcasting Corporation. He also runs the Montreal center of the Brahma Kumaris, and coordinates the activities of this organization in Canada. I think of Eric as one of my best friends. We have known one another for about thirty years, and make it a point to catch up every year.

To my mind, one of Eric's standout qualities is his ability to see the bigger picture. I have the utmost respect and love for him.

I asked Eric, suppose I want to reach out to the twenty-five year old murderer of Toronto, who reportedly had a mental illness. How should I face him and interact with him (or for that matter, how should I face and interact with a terrorist with a firm conviction that his or her calling is to gun down innocents)? Eric's response captured the essence of Marta's story. Read on -

Step one: Accept the aggressor as he or she is.

"Presume that there are no good guys or bad guys," said Eric. If you see an aggressor as a bad person you cannot connect very well. To connect with someone where they are at I cannot judge them. I have to understand their motivation, their intention. Everyone who is fighting is fighting for a cause which they feel is just and right and is meant to be fought. Palestinian against Israelis or Hutus against Tutsis."

"That's a tall order," I said. "Is it possible to see people without judging them?"

"God is a good model," said Eric. "He doesn't see you as good and me as bad. He loves us all."

I smiled and asked Eric if he had ever met a human who was capable of seeing everyone with the same vision?

He thought a bit and added, "Dadi Janki, the present head of the Brahma Kumaris is a good model. She has the ability to see something good in everybody."

Eric shared with me that sometime back, during a discussion on the need to love everyone, Dadi Janki told a group of meditation teachers that when they met someone who did really bad things, they shouldn't have even the slightest memory of a negative emotion connected to what the person did. It should be as if he or she hadn't done anything.

"How inspiring," I said. "What about you? How close have you come to loving everyone?"

"I have worked on myself so I can have at least a little spiritual love for a person I don't like let alone love."

"So if you met a person you didn't like on the street how would you deal with it?" I asked.

"I would respond nicely, kind of as if nothing happened. I would hold my own dignity and self-respect," he answered, and then proceeded to tell me about an episode in his life when a person he knew said a lot of stuff about him on social media.

"That must have been difficult to endure?" I asked.

"Let's say it got me to draw on my decades of experience in meditation and keeping a check on my thoughts. I focused on making him understand that his action had had an impact on me. It created a problem with my work, with my family and with the people around me."

"So today, are you okay with the person?" I asked.

"I hold no grudges, I don't look for apologies, and I don't try to convey to that person (or anyone else who has wronged me) that they are wrong because that would mean judging them. At the most, if I have the opportunity to meet a person to sort out any such issue, I would set out the principles that I believe should be honored in public. I would tell the person that this is serious. But on a spiritual level I love you."

"Seriously? You wouldn't feel hurt at all?"

"I have realized that hurt comes from my own defects, my own weakness that does not allow me to deal with the situation. It has zero to do with what any other person has done. No one gives me sorrow. I take sorrow. The person was just following what he considered to be a good cause for him. He or she is 100% not responsible for my pain or suffering."

I thought about that. I wondered if I would still be able to have empathy with a mentally deranged person if he took up a gun against me, or shot down someone I loved, or with a terrorist who had killed a loved one.

When I was a child, I was very aware that my mother was not mentally sound. She always seemed aloof, somewhat isolated from the world. As if she didn't quite fit in. Her condition got much, much worse after I lost my father, her pillar, when I was in my teens. I vividly remember the day I got back home and she threw a knife at me. This was just before she was formally diagnosed with schizophrenia. I recollect feeling scared about what she might do but never hating her. I used to feel that my mother seemed very lost and very fragile, not of this world at all. When a person gets to that stage of mental disease, aggressive behavior against others is usually the last stop before they harm themselves. I really don't believe I would feel anger against someone who was mentally sick, just extreme sadness.

Terrorism, again, saddens me no end. I wonder what humanity has come to, for people to actually plan to kill other people in the world. Having said that, I'd say it isn't easy to not judge a terrorist and to pin down their aggression to ideology.

I felt I needed more clarity on what makes people violent, so I asked Jayanti, "If someone is violent, what would you say they are experiencing within?"

"Inner conflict," she said. "What's inside gets revealed in my relationships and actions towards others."

Jayanti explained that inner conflict originates when we don't practice what we believe. Every human innately understands and wants love, peace and other virtues. But when we don't express these virtues in what we do, we create inner conflict. So, every time we don't walk the talk, or we don't listen to our conscience, or we listen to our feelings when our conscience is trying to tell us something else, we create conflict inside.

When our inner world is in a state of disarray, we experience no peace and hence cannot connect and communicate positively. We lack self awareness and hence cannot see others with a vision of equality and treat them with dignity.

Jayanti's wisdom suggested that terrorists, murderers and sexual predators, essentially any aggressor, have grown distant from virtues, which made sense. Having lost their way, they expressed no respect for life.

"Okay, so let's assume I have accepted the person as he is. What next?" I asked Eric.

Step two: Think about the space the aggressor is in and see if there's another way to achieve his or her cause, or figure out the best way to steer him/her in the right direction.

Here, Eric underlined the need to act and speak intelligently.

"All the madness that you see in the world comes from a lack of values," he said. "But you can't force values into people's lives. If you try to do that, you're called religiously moralistically dogmatic. If you tell a person who hasn't even started to think about values, or whose ego is very big, that you don't have values, they will say who are you to tell me?"

"So what do you do," I asked Eric.

"Show, don't tell. Find a sophisticated way to show the perpetrator why it's a good idea to be kind. The important thing is they shouldn't feel that you are telling them to be kind. They should just feel that you are giving them an avenue to take benefit from."

"Isn't the best way to show something to be the embodiment of it yourself?"

"Of course, you teach by your actions," agreed Eric. "Say something crazy happens and I stayed patient while everyone got flustered. People would say, Eric is so patient, I can't believe he stayed so cool when that happened. They may then start to have the idea that they would like to be like that instead of get upset. If my behavior and actions are aligned with good values, people will no longer think that you are telling them anything. You will be an embodiment of virtues yourself."

"That sounds pretty cool," I said. But what if the situation were tougher? What if you were in a battle, war zone, and you were sent in to try to get the first level of spiritual intelligence across to the bad guys' camp, say, the terrorists, what would you say or do?"

"I would be better off not telling them not to kill anybody! War may not be the best place to teach spirituality! At the most, if there is some openness, I would talk about the values of dignity, courage and a sense of respect for people around them on the battle field. They may not be the values that will change the war but they are values that may certainly increase the awareness of the person themselves and what they are doing. Don't forget that they may be called bad guys but they are in a war and believe in the cause and have committed to obeying their seniors."

I nodded. I understood what he said very well, after Jayanti's excellent explanation of how inner virtues inform our actions.

Step three: Prepare to be rejected.

"You need understanding and patience for change because transformation is a slow, ongoing process," said Jayanti. "It isn't as if an angel suddenly appears from somewhere and opens up people's hearts.

"You have to keep working on yourself, and working on the world around you, especially on those who seem to be on the brink, to save them from going over. This necessitates staying aware to the people around you so that you can identify those who seem to be getting cut off and lost. Our actions can help save lives."

Can you love your neighbor no matter what he or she does?

It is easy to say we must face the terrorists, murderers and rapists among us but it is one of the hardest things to do. Especially when you think that a spiritually aware person wouldn't need to make an effort to accept someone who has done 'bad' things. He or she would naturally not feel disgust for the negativity in the other.

"Spiritual intelligence means you have maturity, a sort of inner peace so you can be tranquil in stressful situations and see other persons neutrally even if they have other views," said my friend Elisabeth Angeby Hesslefors when I interviewed her for this book. "The word equanimity comes to mind, which is essentially calmness and composure, especially in a difficult situation. Only then would your spiritual intelligence help make the world a better place."

"How would you define maturity?" I asked.

"Maturity means you can respect the dignity of every person even if they have been doing bad things," she said.

I was impressed.

If you had asked me if I knew anyone with an all-embracing view on humanity, I would have identified Elisabeth. Let me detract for a moment and tell you a little about her.

Elisabeth retired as a senior lecturer at the University of Gothenburg in 2011 after a lifetime of teaching and travelling. I was introduced to her at a meditation retreat in India through her husband Ragnar Angeby, a former diplomat with the Swedish Ministry of Foreign Affairs, Sweden's ambassador to Romania in the mid nineties, and current advisor to the Folke Bernadotte Academy, a Swedish agency for peace, security and development. Elisabeth and I became friends through our chats on life.

Coming back to our interview, I was curious to know how Elisabeth would suggest achieving that state of maturity.

"Elisabeth", I said, "if you are talking about acceptance, I assume you've achieved it to a greater degree than most of us. Can you tell me how you developed this vision?"

Elisabeth shared an anecdote from her early working days.

"When I was being trained as a primary school teacher, I was focused on the role of a teacher in the education system, what you say, how you behave, what teaching materials you use and so on," she said.

"When I started working, I remember this moment during my first job... one of my pupils was a twin with learning difficulties. While seeing the student struggle I had an epiphany. I realized that my chosen profession was not about me, it was about my pupils.

"In that moment I realized that a good teacher has to be interested in pupils, in their learning difficulties, and in finding ways to help them overcome those challenges. You could say my vision started to broaden."

"Disciplining pupils was a learning curve as well," she continued.

"I see," I said.

"You had to be watchful to be a catalyst to help them learn."

"Years later my first trip out of Europe was to Vietnam in 1983, where my former husband was helping to establish a paper mill to manufacture paper for school books," she continued. "Later, a Vietnamese minister of education and her assistant and one headmaster visited Sweden as part of a study tour that my former husband and I organized. In 1987, I visited India to conduct field studies. Then I visited South Africa on an exchange program and the USA."

"My travel was not about having a good time," she said. "It was focused on understanding people and learning about other cultures, and in the process, getting to know myself and my culture better."

"Can you describe how conducting a field study helped you learn about yourself and your culture?" I asked.

"Well, when you interact with other people you need to be outspoken. You need to be very clear about your own values so that necessitates you to question yourself."

"And how did these exposures help broaden your vision?" I asked.

"While engaging with people I realized that the field study was not about what I was experiencing in their presence but about their experiences, their struggles, their thought processes and so on. I must understand what someone else is going through to appreciate their point of view. Maturity has its roots in being able to see things from another's perspective."

"So, as I gather, one of the first necessities of becoming more spiritually intelligent is to stay open to anything that can expand your horizon," I said.

"Of course," agreed Elisabeth. "Being narrow-minded is not a sign of being spiritually intelligent."

A gentleman I interviewed, Colonel Raj Pawah, a former military man, an engineer and motivational speaker with a keen interest in spirituality, had only one thing to say about spiritual intelligence, and that was to emphasize that individual perception is the root cause of every problem in this world.

"We all have our own way of looking at things based on our upbringing, value systems and other parameters," he said. "We look at things the way we want to look at things. That is what we call perception. The problem starts when our perception differs from another's and we assume that the other person is wrong and I am right.

"If we could understand the others' viewpoint as well as our own, half of the world's problems would end, and here I'm talking of problems between individuals as well as problems between countries."

"Half the world's problems, you say?"

"Half of the problems will vanish when we understand that the other person is different and not wrong," said the Colonel.

"What steps do people need to take to understand the word perception?" I asked.

"We need to learn to be receptive. The problem is we are very talkative. We just don't listen. We're wonderful speakers but terrible listeners. We have a mouth that can be closed and two ears that cannot. I think that suggests that God made us with the intention that we listen more than we speak. But we do the opposite. We need listening skills. We need to listen with our heart and soul to understand the other person's point of view."

"Where does ego come in all this?" I asked.

"Believing that 'my perception is right' is an expression of ego. You can only truly listen when you put your ego aside. Perception is your mind's interpretation of reality. It may be reality, it may not be reality."

I could identify with what Elisabeth and Colonel Raj said.

When I first started travelling, it was as a tourist, as many people travel. I travelled to have a good time. I travelled to enjoy good weather, to see great places and to meet new people. I can't really say I travelled to enjoy different cuisines because I'm anything but a foodie!

Over the years, my yearning to travel hasn't diminished at all but my motivation for travel has certainly changed.

I now travel to get under the skin of places and people, so to speak. I travel to learn about distant communities and their lifestyles and the challenges they face. I try to become a part of the community while I travel, which Elisabeth said is very important.

Travel has certainly helped open my eyes to many truths. It has helped me understand other people's perceptions and realize how important it is to set aside my own perceptions. I consider myself privileged for that opportunity. However, it is not as if you have to travel to grow as a human.

And you? When will you begin that long journey into yourself?

Wise words by Rumi, the great Sufi poet and mystic, wouldn't you agree?

"You need to be open to learning," reiterated Elisabeth, and she made it very clear that nowadays, almost everyone is sufficiently exposed to the rest of the world, through social media, to imbibe life lessons from paying attention to what is happening in other parts and understand the impact on human life and the environment.

And even if you don't have access to social media, she said, you still have different kinds of people around you.

Essentially, we are surrounded by people with divergent opinions no matter where we live. The big question is have we grown enough to accept those with divergent opinions in our own backyard?

I'll sign off with a reference to the Bible. The command to 'love your neighbor as yourself' is found eight times in the Bible. Not once. Not twice. Eight times.

Hmm.

God made 'love your neighbor as yourself' a command because He knew we'd struggle. With an open mind and sensitivity that struggle will ease.

A spiritual approach to climate change

I'm in Newfoundland to spend time with friends. Walking in surroundings that I love, I found myself looking around and wondering which areas might be affected the most by climate change.

Canada is one of several places in the world bearing the brunt of climate change. The world has warmed by one degree Celsius in the last 135 years, but in parts of Canada, the temperature has crept up in some seasons by four to five degrees Celsius in the last seventy years, according to Environment Canada's senior climatologist, David Phillips. That's twice as much in half the time.

To come back to my present surroundings, Canada's Changing Climate, a report out earlier this year, observed that Nova Scotia and Prince Edward Island, and parts of New Brunswick and the island of Newfoundland, would experience between 75 cm and 100 cm sea level rise during the coming century, exacerbating the risk of flooding and loss of property and, grim as it sounds, the loss of life, during storm surges.

A month ago I was at a conference (Spirit of Humanity) in Iceland where Jayanti delivered a stern message. Every corner of the world is in the same boat insofar as the environment is concerned. If we don't deal with the environment, we will sink together.

I met up with four old friends some days before this conference. We spent lunch talking about the mess in the world and what did I think would happen?

My friends understood that the environment was a mess but they hoped it could be corrected or turned around. When I said I didn't think that that could happen, they got upset.

Now I'm no cynic but what makes me doubt the possibility of our getting our act together is the fact that I honestly feel it is too late. Everything is escalating at great speed but governments just aren't acting the way they should be.

I vividly remember a visit to Greenland twelve years ago. I was in a hotel with two Huskies sitting at my feet. Outside the window, I had a clear view of melting ice. It was seventy degrees Fahrenheit in July, which was very hot by Greenland standards, and I was thinking 'Why don't people get it? It's not rocket science'.

When I shared this with Marta, she told me she could remember visiting appliance repair shops (I think they don't exist anymore but this anecdote is from decades ago) in her childhood with her mother.

"We would get the iron repaired if it malfunctioned. The TV repaired. And so on. Today, the trend is to trash malfunctioning electrical and electronics and buy new ones," she said.

"If you love nature you will think ten times - and some more - before you use any resource," she said.

I nodded and continued to think out loud. "How do you teach people? You can't take them all to Greenland. To my mind, if you see a documentary on any of these places it should be clear enough. But I've never been able to figure out why people don't get it."

"When I got home from Greenland and told the people around me that the globe was in trouble, they thought I was kidding. But no, global warming was happening. It still is."

"The future of the planet as a place where humanity can flourish is empirically at risk," agreed Will.

"I think this is truly a sobering time in the history of humanity," he said. "We are facing complex challenges on a planetary scale, particularly the environmental question but also related to it the use of resources, the devastation through drought, famine, war in large parts of the world that are forcing migration with all the resultant challenges that that raises. And into that context we are looking for leadership at all levels of society and around the world but particularly leadership at an institutional level that is able to operate on a large scale and for the long term.

"We need institutions of great integrity because it is through institutions that we are able to organize on a larger scale beyond the individual initiative or charismatic impact of a particular person.

"The problem is, from the 1960s onwards through the generations we grew up in North America and Europe and around the world there has been a general disillusionment in institutions at all levels, in their authority, in our trust in them and in their viability," Will said. "And the reason for that disillusionment is the lack of systematic leadership at the institutional level.

"Where are the people with spiritual intelligence who understand the complexity and the urgency of this challenge to the planet, and all the dimensions of the environmental crisis, but who will think beyond their immediate self interests and take decisions with an eye on the long term?"

Truly, where are those people?

In conversation with Glynis, my friend who lives in Majorca, I lamented the lack of political leadership, talking down leaders such as Trump and others who are just about self-interest.

"Well, don't forget we are the one who vote those politicians in," she said.

I sat bolt upright. Trust Glynis to bring the discussion back to where we can make a difference. She is blunt. I know her directness has ruffled feathers on many an occasion. I welcomed the nudge.

"We've all got to make changes, haven't we?" she said.

I let her have her say.

"Every one of us who buys into shopping on Amazon or insists on shopping on a Sunday, we are the ones who don't want to change our easy comfortable shopping habits. We don't want to grow it. We don't want to kill it. We want it all to be very easy.

"We aren't interested in who is cleaning wherever we go, how much they are getting paid. We want to take home millions of dollars a year just for being the head of a company (or some top spot) and accepting that some workers can live in their car in the car park (or in a tiny space you could hardly call a home) while you keep racking up.

"We're all part and parcel to the mess in the environment if we don't say 'Hang on a minute, why is that employee living in the car park'?"

"So, you're saying we need to step back and evaluate our own lives?" I asked.

"There can be no change in the world without us realizing, what's my part in it? And to realize that, we need to stop and consider what's happening around us," she said. "We need to ask that question not just once but every day and every moment."

"Is realizing our part enough to prompt change?" I asked.

"Well, to change you need a shift in perspective. And to right the current wrong, you would need a major shift in perspective. You would need to understand that the lifestyle we have bought into isn't sustainable."

"Because we've become very materialistic, right?" I clarified.

"Yes, mainly because we have stopped thinking about the impact of our choices on the world. Consider tourism. We've got millions of tourists coming into Majorca, people who have bought into the idea marketed so well by travel companies 'You've earned yourself a holiday'. They feel 'Yes, it is my right to go on holiday'.

"Well, yes, but what are you buying into when you do that?

"Do they think about the consequences of their holidaying in Majorca? Do any of us think about the consequences of travelling too much? Consuming too much, or patronizing unsustainable business patterns? But we all insist on going on holiday. When I was growing up, we didn't 'go' on holiday. But we enjoyed our holiday all the same."

I nodded.

I was reminded of a news report I recently read about trash littering the snowy ascent to Mount Everest. Tents, empty oxygen tanks, climbing equipment, food containers and human waste are defiling what once used to be pristine surroundings. But with the number of people scaling the 29,000 feet peak rising to a record 800 in 2018 (as against the nearly 5,000 mountaineers who have ascended since Edmund Hillary and Tenzing Norgay first did in 1953, that is, over the last sixty-six years), the amount of trash left behind has grown manifold of late. Clearly, adventure seekers aren't thinking about the consequences of their jaunts.

Life was simpler when I was growing up, before I became very consumerist myself. I thank my travels for having opened my eyes to the mess in the environment.

Yes, I am aware that travelling is a burden on the world. One of my takeaways from my conversation with Will was about the nature of power, about how to use influence in a good way and not just use people and/or resources. I have gradually realized that it is essential to influence what you can. Every small step in the world counts.

I used to be a daily avid shopper at the mall. Now I shop only for what I need, and try to get in and out as quickly as possible.

My fondness for art and beautiful furniture got the better of me for many years in my life. I finally took a stand at the age of seventy, when I let go most of my stuff, my cars and my fancy clothes - although I must confess, cashmere sweaters are a weakness. I still love beautiful things and appreciate them in the homes of other people but I no longer need to own them. I have whittled down my possessions to fit into nine to ten suitcases, which are parked around the world.

And I no longer have a permanent place to call home! I grew up believing that bigger is better in terms of the size of a home. Homes in Canada and the US are larger than those in Europe. Since I started to travel, I've seen very small homes where nothing is missing, and people are happy with less.

As Glynis said, saving the planet is about saving ourselves and it needs us to question, question, question, every facet of our life.

"We have a moral responsibility to the generations after us. We trashed the place," said Will.

I couldn't agree more.

And that takes me to one last point.

It is very easy to feel disillusioned by the increasing number of extreme climatic events that are causing untold suffering in every corner of the world. It is easy to think we have crossed a point of no return and therefore, feel it is useless to do anything about the situation - at the individual level or at the level of the community.

When I interviewed Jayanti, she described the present time as one of 'descending energy' because we can see the world becoming more violent, more aggressive, more materialistic, being stripped of natural resources, more climate chaos and so on. I appreciated her frankness. I also appreciated the energy in the voice and in the way she lives her life.

That led me to ask if she has always felt optimistic. Don't you ever get depressed about the tiny steps we are taking to save the planet and the ongoing march of climate change?

Jayanti told me that in the early eighties, when she was first exposed to climate and associated information about the world at conferences of the United Nations, which she attended as a representative of the Brahma Kumaris, she got upset to hear scientists speak about humanity having gone beyond the point of no return, in the case of climate change.

"I would feel very hopeless about it all," she said.

However, spirituality helped her understand that there is a widespread planetary transformation hidden in extreme climatic events and natural calamities.

"To use a metaphor, it is night time for the world," she said. "This night will come to an end and a new day will begin. However, as long as the night is ongoing, we will see hardship. I feel happy to think that a better world for all lies ahead, not too far away."

"So you are convinced about the world changing for the better?"

"Yes, the number of people who are incorporating spirituality into their life, not for ten minutes a day but such that it impacts everything they do including their choices that impact the environment, may still be a minority but the power of this minority will grow in the near future because we are passing through a time of transformation. I am convinced that the tipping point is near."

What has spirituality got to do with leadership?

Our world is in turmoil. There's hardly a country left where either the economy or the society is not in a mess. Here I am thinking, when a crisis arises, the first thing people look for is a leader.

But, the world is facing a crisis of leadership. In a previous chapter on climate change, Will identified the lack of systematic leadership at the institutional level as being one of the reasons for the lack of action in protecting the environment. Climate change is one area where we're seeing the impact of weak leadership. Developing inclusive policies is another area leaders are failing people in.

Upkar identified society's drifting away from the spiritual principles of universality, compassion and empathy - seeing people who are different from us as 'the other' rather than part of us, as something that has been exacerbated by political, governmental, business and religious leaders. Some of these individuals, who are supposed to be beacons - pointing us in the right direction and inspiring us to do better as human beings - are instead using their platforms to condone or foment fear, sexism, dishonesty, divisiveness and racism.

While no leader is perfect, if I think of leaders I look up to, Winston Churchill comes to mind for being tough and simultaneously vulnerable in the sense that he agonized when he knew people would suffer at the consequences of his decisions.

Another name is Mohandas Karamchand Gandhi for his

compassion for the common man.

I can add Pierre Trudeau, the late former prime minister of Canada, for opening up the country to a multicultural policy, which I think reflects an astute understanding of the need for creating conditions for acceptance and belonging.

In more recent times, one leader that stands out for me is Angela Merkel. She demonstrated courage in the face of criticism and condemnation for her stance on migrants. She did not capitulate to political expediency but anchored her actions in her humanity. Her strength of character, her competence and her communication skills built credibility and trust. But she is an exception. Leaders on the world stage who are able to retain their integrity in the face of pressure are few and far between.

What's wrong with our society that we aren't producing leaders who think beyond their power games, for the benefit of people and the environment?

Nirwair had an interesting take.

"All the leaders have very big aspirations," he said.

"Do you mean egos?" I asked.

"Ego comes later," he said. "Every President elected in America has been elected because people had high hopes from the person, be it President Trump, Barack Obama, Bill Clinton and so on, and I believe those leaders genuinely wanted to do something for their people."

"Hmm," I said.

"But those leaders are human beings and they are also stuck in their own limited way of thinking. Whatever change they could initiate, if at all, was temporary. They could not bring the stability that people seek."

"That is true," I agreed. But I also feel that some of the leaders we see today are simply not inclusive in their vision. As I see it, one of the foremost traits of a leader is an understanding of people hailing from all walks of life - not just those who match your religion or economic status or lifestyle - and being fair to all. I know this is easier said than done, but it is a frontier a leader has to cross.

I've written a lot about understanding people in a previous chapter, even understanding those who commit acts that we see as evil, such as setting off bombs or rape. My exchange with Elisabeth hopefully yielded some practical tips on understanding people.

I also gained a valuable tip about understanding people from Dr Partap Midha, a doctor who has led the J Watumull Global Hospital & Research Center, a medium size hospital in Mount Abu, in northwest India, since its inception in 1991. As an aside, I have visited Mount Abu maybe thirty times in the last three decades. I first met Dr Partap during one such visit soon after the hospital had started operations. I had fallen sick with pneumonia and needed to be admitted to the hospital. I think I was the first Western patient to be hospitalized. Another doctor Vinay Laxmi cared for me and when I recovered, she showed me around the villages around Mount Abu which had no medical facilities, which she visited to offer free consultations. I was very inspired to do something to help people and went on to create a charity that funded several small projects of the hospital and many other initiatives around the world. I worked with Dr Partap and Vinay on these projects. Vinay sadly passed away about a decade ago.

Dr Partap is one of the most humble men I have ever met. His respect for humanity and genuine desire to help the less fortunate are noteworthy.

In conversation with me, he said, "You need to really listen to people, observe them. What are they trying to convey? Often, we react without listening. Unless you really hear what people are saying, you can't connect with people let alone understand them."

But listening is an art. I quoted Krishnamurti on listening in my chapter on free thinking - to catch what is being said to you, to get the feeling behind words spoken to you, and to truly know what is happening around, to engage with the world meaningfully, you need to listen without filters.

Dr Partap suggested developing the ability to stay silent and patient, to improve your listening skills.

Silence and patience lie in the spiritual domain as do other virtues that help understand people and connect with them.

Consider - only someone who has understood love and experienced love will be able to understand people, express compassion and empathy, and forgive.

Only someone with a practice of faith can check their ego at the door, which is so essential when you enter the public arena.

What I'm getting at is, someone who has assessed himself or herself, who has worked on himself or herself, is best positioned to reflect the values of a leader. This came out very strongly in conversation with Marie-Lise How Fok Cheung, a friend of mine in Mauritius.

When I first met Marie-Lise about five years ago, she was the senior chief executive of the ministry of health in Mauritius, a very high position where she had about 13,000 people working under her. She came across as self assured, very capable and with a strong value system.

Marie-Lise has since retired but she was still someone who I definitely wanted to interview for this book. Interestingly, and perhaps expectedly, her sharing on spiritual intelligence was a strong message on leadership.

Although she described her operational environment as highly bureaucratic, a place 'where firmness was warranted', she professed to relying strongly on her meditation practice to understand herself better, develop skills to reach out and help others, and wherever possible, to replace rigid procedures with creativity and flexibility.

"Through Raja Yoga meditation I connected with the divine," she said. "I felt His support and discovered my inner strength. It helped mould how I approached circumstances."

"Can you please share a few examples of how meditation helped you?" I requested.

"Sure," she said. "My daily practice of listening to my inner voice through meditation helped me open up to the minister (my political boss), my staff and listen to their inner feelings and needs, thus giving them a sense of self worth and motivation in whatever they did.

"Meditation taught me to use my heart as well as my head, that is, bring empathy, compassion and sensitivity to daily management."

In my chapter on free thinking, David said, "In the challenging times we live in, people will look to someone who they see as being connected for assistance. It helps the world to become spiritually streetwise, if I may put it that way."

By being connected, he meant knowing what to do even when, or especially when the world around you is going up in flames. That suggests having a very, very well developed power of intuition. I found it interesting that Marie-Lise narrated how meditation helped develop her intuitive power.

"In circumstances and in jobs that demanded that I sharpen my intuitive skills, I achieved this by going in silence for a few minutes," she said.

Again, the power of silence!

"Can you describe how the intuition came in handy?" I asked.

"Intuition in managerial decision-making and problem solving offers the potential for greater innovation, particularly when dealing with situations in which precedents are unclear," she said. "Intuition helped me take sound decisions that were not always based solely on the basis of rationality but on a combination of logic and intuition."

In my opinion, facilitation is another key trait of a leader. It means seeing the bigger picture and having the ability to make things happen notwithstanding any opposition.

Marie-Lise described using her interpersonal skills in influence to manage amidst coalitions and opposition. She relied on her high sense of tactfulness and inner resilience to withstand politically motivated agendas.

"Did you ever find it depressing to navigate politically charged environments? Say, if you had to compromise on your values?"

"Here is a secret - I always went by my core values. I always strived to be true to myself, to be aligned with my truth. While maintaining my truth, I learned to develop a kind of flexibility," she said.

An anecdote that Will shared also highlighted how a person pushed into a leadership position can dig deep to find the resilience to face tough situations.

Will described what he called 'a dark moment' in his career when, as a minister, he chaired a major board of the General Assembly of the Church of Scotland.

"I led my board to adopt a certain course of action that I felt reflected integrity and effectiveness," he described.

"I gather it wasn't the easy action," I asked.

"No, it wasn't. In fact, a well-wisher said to me 'You're a popular person and you're used to being liked. Well, now you're going to find yourself subjected to a lot of hate. Can you face that?'"

"That was tough," I said.

"It was. He also said, 'Whatever holds your life together, is it strong enough to hold your life together now, in the face of this leadership challenge?'"

"That is a great takeaway for any leader," I remarked. "Whatever holds your life together, is it strong enough to hold your life together when you have to stand up for what is right? I think if you are made of the right stuff you will take the right position, I reflected. You will not be able to do otherwise."

"If it is inside you, it will come out," opined Will.

"Precisely," I said. "If I might ask, what helped you tide over the situation?"

"The love and brave support of my wife and a few people I hardly knew - our mutual friend Georgie Baxendale above all - who stood by me, they helped," continued Will. "A lot of people I thought were friends who would give me the benefit of the doubt when they heard about the controversy in fact turned away and believed my critics, and that was an awakening as well."

"Ah!" I said. "You must have learned who are the people who are important?"

"Yes. Also, what really helped was a deeper reliance on my own Christian faith. I discovered the depth of the tradition that my life is based on, spiritual resources, if you will, that could guide a person through any leadership crises: above all the wisdom of the Psalms and the Gospels.

"Do you know, Betty, the spirituality of the Psalms and the stories of the Gospels are all about struggling to do the right thing in the face of hostility."

"How interesting," I remarked.

"I also learned compassion," he said.

"How's that?" I asked.

"Well, I was calling on people to stand by the decision on institutional change that we had made together and not everyone did under pressure. Some people turned and ran or changed sides when the church establishment rose in opposition to the change on the floor of the General Assembly."

"You didn't feel bad about that," I asked?

"A colleague said to me 'Some of the anger in people who aren't with you is just about security'. I realized that a lot of people simply couldn't take the pressure to stand with me, even when I won the vote in the General Assembly to continue with the reforms that the establishment wanted to stop.

"That taught me that a leader has to be caring about those around. You have to understand that the heat is too strong for some people and we should not be judgmental about that."

*

I think that Marie-Lise's and Will's sharing bring home the point that you can acquire the traits of a good leader, that leaders are made and not necessarily born.

What's that you're thinking?

Why should I bother?

Allow me to share an anecdote to tell you why I believe we need to develop leadership skills.

Activist and actor Russell Brand interviewed journalist and author Sarah Wilson on the need to transition from being purely spiritual to engaging with the world.

She mentioned the adage of the monk coming down from the mountain, which I really liked, and she shared a valuable story from her latest book, First, We Make the Beast Beautiful.

Sarah had the opportunity to ask the Dalai Lama one question. She agonized over what to ask and ended up asking, "How do I get my mind to shut up?"

The Dalai Lama's response was, "Silly! Impossible to achieve! If you can do it, great. If not, big waste of time."

"But surely you can do it?" said Sarah.

"Noooo. If I sit in a cave for a year on mountain, then maybe I do it. But no guarantee. Anyway, I don't have time."

The Dalai Lama told Sarah he had better things to do like teaching altruism to massive crowds around the world. He told her he had recently been to Japan and other places where he had addressed audiences of thousands.

Sarah realized that if the Dalai Lama had figured out the value of service, she needed to think about it as well.

The essence of this, to quote Sarah, is if we are aware, we need to get down and dirty and share the message. We need to lead from the front.

This came up in conversation with Marilyn. She is a fairly private person and confessed that she doesn't like being pushed into the public space but her work (as a psychic) requires her to face large audiences of up to 2,000 people.

"Once in a while I get overwhelmed by the volume of people seeking my services," she said. "A part of me is not comfortable with being in public spaces while another part of me understands that if I can help heal one person, if I can nurse one soul and give the person a peaceful night, then my work is worth it.

"I see influence as an important role to play," she said. "I think it is important to become a person of influence."

"Can you explain that?" I requested.

"Have you read the book Becoming a Person of Influence?" she asked.

I nodded.

"It describes how to positively impact the lives of those you have the privilege of leading and developing. It is up to spiritually aware people to influence others into being well and whole and happy. It is up to us to make them aware that there is more to life than just sitting and having drinks and a meal together. Wouldn't that be a wonderful group to have on this planet?"

Indeed, it would!

PART FIVE

When is it the right time to work on yourself?

When I set out to understand spiritual intelligence, I was sure that one of the people I wanted to interview was Margaret, a lady who I admire very much. Nowadays Margaret is widely known for being the mother of Justin Trudeau, the incumbent Canadian prime minister. However, when I first met her in the early eighties, she was better known for being a former first lady. Margaret had three children with Pierre Elliott Trudeau, the prime minister of Canada at the time.

In her own right, Margaret is an accomplished author, actress, photographer, former television talk show hostess and a social advocate for people with bipolar disorder, a condition she has long suffered from.

I wanted to interview Margaret for this book because she has seen it all and survived to tell the tale. It seemed to me that someone whose spirit has prevailed over multiple hardships and yet, and this is a key point, has not hardened, for she is a very loving person, and who has held onto her zest for life, would definitely have something valuable to share about facing life's challenges.

Margaret's and my first encounter in a hotel lobby in the eighties happened soon after she had separated from Pierre. She was struggling to get by in those days. Pierre and she were sharing custody of their three children but she wasn't getting any alimony. It didn't help that she was heavily into drugs, a habit she had picked up during the later years of her marriage, for which the media came down hard on her. In those days I felt very sorry for Margaret. I knew she was dating the likes of Ted Kennedy, Mick Jagger and Jack Nicholson, and that she hung out with many celebrities in night clubs in New York and London. But she didn't seem happy.

Domesticity and a semblance of normalcy crept back into Margaret's life after her remarriage, in 1984, to Fred Kemper, a real estate developer. She had two more children with him. But true happiness continued to elude her.

Why?

She still hadn't figured out her purpose in life. In an interview to Macleans (a popular Canadian magazine) in 2010, Margaret recollected her mindset in 1998, a time when she believed her 'usefulness was finished'.

"I believed my job on Earth was to procreate and be a pleasant sexual diversion for hard-working men."

That low was nothing as compared to what came next. After the tragic loss of one of her sons (Michel Trudeau) in a skiing accident in 1998, Margaret slipped into a depression that cost her her second marriage. She divorced Fred in 1999. The following year was equally tough on her. Pierre was shattered by Michel's death. He couldn't take the loss.

"You don't want to live after your son dies. You just don't. Pierre couldn't," Margaret told Macleans in 2010.

When Pierre passed away, Margaret was at his bedside with their two surviving sons Justin and Alexandre. "Just because our marriage ended didn't mean the love stopped," she said.

With Pierre gone, Margaret was left alone to handle her grief.

The loneliness became unbearable, plunging her into the depths of drug abuse and despair. She wanted to follow her little boy. To quote her from Macleans, "I didn't want to be alone. In my grief I was so focused on the loss of my boy that I forgot that I had a full life and lots of people who love me very much who are alive and well and here."

When I asked her about that time of her life, Margaret said, "I had absolutely no gratitude for the wonder that was still in my life."

We were chatting over the phone; the energy in her voice was palpable.

"What helped turnaround your situation?" I asked.

"Definitely the health services," she said. "You can't fix yourself by yourself. Take help. Medicine and the right care can do a lot for you. I can't emphasize that enough."

I could relate to that. I was in my teens when my mother was diagnosed with schizophrenia. She was better when she was on medication. When she stopped her medication, which was often because she had no clue of what she was doing, she became practically unmanageable.

Looking back, I could say that a person knowledgeable about mental health would have seen my mother heading for a breakdown. Throughout my childhood I had known her to be too quiet. I had just thought she was very introverted and overly dependent on her husband. Actually, she had probably lived on the brink for many years until my father's early death pushed her over.

Margaret couldn't emphasize enough the need to focus on healing when the going is good to avoid falling to pieces when the going gets tough. I loved that.

"So when the going is good, you think we still aren't doing okay?" I asked.

"Many of us (like me) aren't self aware. We don't know who we are, what makes us happy and where we fit in," she said. "What are the words you're using, spiritual intelligence? To be aware of yourself is to be spiritually intelligent. You have to face your demons and find sustainable solutions to your problems to feel well."

"And as you say, this process of figuring out life is best done when life seems okay?"

"Yes," she said. "When a big thing comes, if you are not well, you will be taken for a ride. You will needlessly face highs and lows. Essentially, you will lose your balance very easily."

"Is that what happened to you?"

Margaret rued, "For so many years, my manic mind didn't serve me but I wasn't ready to come out and tell the world I was suffering. I tried to fix my condition on my own. Some of those who suffer as I did choose alcohol, some choose cannabis, either is just a means to ease physical and emotional pain."

"Did it help?" I asked.

"It often pulled me out of brooding over past hurts and into the now, in the positive, beautiful world I live in today. But no, it didn't cure me."

Margaret was not referring to her depression but to her long struggle with bipolar disease. She was hospitalized for emotional stress as early as the mid seventies but she did not get the medical help she needed until much later. Bipolar episodes happen when the hormones serotonin and dopamine are unbalanced. There is good pharmaceutical medication that corrects this imbalance and gives you back the opportunity to live a good life.

Margaret has been doing much better since she publicly announced her diagnosis in 2006. Since then, she has avidly campaigned for reducing the social stigma of mental disease, to tell people that the mentally ill shouldn't be admitted to homes that are horrible places to be in. A point of reference - the hospital in the award winning movie One Flew Over the Cuckoo's Nest. It wasn't far-fetched. It was a fairly accurate depiction of the state of mental hospitals. I've seen homes for the mentally sick first-hand and they are places with a sad vibe. It is needless. With proper care, a person can gain control on mental disease and even overcome it.

The woman in front of me had worked on herself and that was what counted. She was in control now.

"Life's problems never die. What do you do to hang on to your sanity now?" I asked.

"I experienced five years of anger after my son died before I felt joy," she said. "That is a long time. Now that I've figured out where I fit in, I stay in that space. I stay connected with who I am," she said. "That awareness keeps me grounded. It protects me from being carried away by negative momentum."

Is your spirituality for show?
Or has it become a part of you?

I have a friend Claire Dunphy, now going strong in her eighties. When I first met her on a mountain top in Australia in the early nineties, she was chanting and waving feathers in front of graves in the rocks. I thought she was quite mad!

Strangely, we hit it off. I say strangely because I no longer engage with feathers or crystals or candles in the hope of achieving enlightenment through them. Years ago, all of these tools, if I may call them so, adorned my book shelves. I gave them away because they never worked for me, unlike my friend Michael, who uses crystals very effectively to connect with the divine and because doing so gives him a very good feeling and helps him make decisions. When I interviewed him, he reminded me that the ancient rabbis used to use crystals to communicate with God, a practice that disappeared after the sixth century AD. Michael also reminded me of Hebrew prayers that help prepare one to use crystals to ask questions and watch or listen for answers, for the simple reason that unless your lines are clear and open, you cannot hear the divine.

"Crystals help me decide whether what I'm doing is appropriate, and once I have decided I take responsibility for all my decisions," he said.

Since time immemorial humanity has needed stepping stones to reach something deeper. Centuries ago, I understand that the Saint

Augustine used to encourage some seekers to go on pilgrimages to holy places like the shrines of the martyrs, despite the fact that he emphasized that the true pilgrimage is an ascent of the self to God, essentially, a conversion of the self.

Apparently, Augustine believed that worldly elements, in the sense of a physical pilgrimage, can be useful to some people because in general, we can understand the material world more easily than heavenly things. However, lest every seeker set off on a pilgrimage, he made it clear that physical pilgrimage was not strictly necessary for spiritual pilgrimage.

What you really need is the will to look within and work on yourself until it becomes obvious that you own spirituality. To get back to Claire, I think what worked for us was during the week that we lived together in the bush (Australian for outdoors away from cities) I got to know her for who she truly was. Despite her maverick ways, she is one of the wisest souls I know who really does walk the talk. That means a lot to me.

I was chatting to Eric about this and he came up with an excellent analogy of spiritual innocence versus spiritual intelligence.

"Spirituality can be a bit like a nice little joint of cannabis that creates a cloud in your head that makes you see the world in a positive way," he said. "It makes you optimistic. It helps you to connect with beautiful values, love, peace and happiness, and makes you want to bring some goodness into the world."

I smiled. "That sounds good," I said.

"You're right. It will make you sound good. It will make you feel good. But that is about it. You will not be effective in implementing those good intentions."

"Why," I asked.

"Because to be truly spiritual, or, if I may say so, to be spiritually intelligent, you need to align your intentions with your attitude and your behavior. To be spiritually intelligent is to embody values in a very practical way. Say, you have a good intention. I'm going to bring peace on earth. Well good luck to you. But then you go judge people, complain about everyone, criticize this one and that one, think you are better than everyone. Then your behavior becomes a little bit arrogant, egotistical, and even defamatory to a certain extent."

"You call this spiritual innocence because spirituality is nowhere in the picture?" I asked.

"Yes, because it is a little bit innocent, like a child who has no experience in life. Like a child who crossed the road without knowing that he would get hit by a passing truck, he wasn't stupid, he just didn't know about the world."

"And in contrast to that, someone who is spiritually intelligent would be walking the talk?"

"Yes. Essentially, you have allowed your interest in spirituality to blossom. You have developed wisdom, which allows you to apply that spirituality to your day-to-day life. Your attitude and behavior match your intentions."

"Say someone is spiritually innocent. Say, they have started to think about spirituality but are still caught up with frills like buying a fancy yoga mat and all that. Isn't something better than nothing?" I asked.

"You're asking about the type who drinks green tea," Eric said.

"Whatever," I said.

"Not really," said Eric. "Spiritual innocence goes out of the window in a flash when a challenging situation comes about. People who are just nice, innocently spiritual can't face powerful situations or they will face it but not with their spirituality, just with their normal humanity."

"So, how would someone who is spiritually intelligent face a challenge?"

"Their spirituality is lasting, it has become them, it is always theirs to use. Essentially, you can't claim to have spiritual intelligence. If you have it, it will show through. You will demonstrate it. Those who are spiritually intelligent will have a clear head even when they are confronted with very serious issues. Their intellect will stay clear. Their spirituality is not intellectual; it is not academic; it is not dogmatic; it is not religious. It is pure wisdom. It is rooted in values."

"Have you always been spiritually intelligent, Eric?" I asked.

"No. I nurtured good intentions about myself for a long time. I wanted to become a better person. I wanted to transform the world. But my behavior was not optimum."

"So what nudged you into aligning your intentions with your behavior?"

"Spiritual intelligence eventually came after some very heavy confrontations with reality," he said.

"Can you please elaborate that a bit?"

"Well, you know what you are told. Anger is bad, you should not be angry. A good person doesn't get angry."

I smiled.

"So I tried not to get angry," he continued. "I would repress my anger. But you know what? I couldn't keep it up forever. One day, my anger exploded like a bomb."

"What happened?" I asked.

"I was angry about something. I was wearing a T-shirt and when I got home and tried to remove it, I pulled so hard that it ripped."

"Wow!" I chuckled.

"I felt foolish. This was after having practicing meditation for ten years. Eric, I thought, if the person you are mad with was in front of you, you might have just punched him in the face."

"How true," I said.

"I could have hidden behind my feelings but that day, I chose to face my anger. I accepted that my meditation hadn't done enough for me. So there must have been something I was not doing well, or well enough. Something was missing. That day I realized that I was innocent about spirituality. I had a good intention, I wanted to stay peaceful, but I was not going deep enough to change myself."

"You were just drinking green tea," I remarked.

Eric smiled. "You could say that. But spirituality involves facing your demons, your ugliness. It necessitates being really patient, accepting that you may be totally wrong about everything, being ready to start from scratch."

"So what you are saying is that change doesn't happen overnight, it takes time and effort."

"Yes, and it also takes honesty and courage because there will be times when you fall flat on your face in the mud. You will have to lift yourself up and face the world with all that mud on your face and clean up your act, sometimes in full view of the world."

"That's excellent," I said. "So we basically need to face ourselves. If I might ask, what role does God play in this, if at all?"

"I see intelligence as a kind of energy. I have seen spiritually intelligent people pick up signs from Nature and from God. When I am spiritually intelligent, I accept that truth will not emerge in my head. It will come from an external pure source. That is God."

"And that is why you meditate to pick up signs?"

"Yes, to commune with God."

"This may be a silly question but do you think any effort can be achieved in a certain time-frame? Suppose you decide you want to overcome anger. Can you set a date to achieving that?"

"It isn't a silly question. I think the timeline depends on the intensity of your effort. You have to be serious about your transformation. In the path I have chosen, we are advised volcanic yoga to work on any stubborn habits. You need to look for both the gross and the subtle signs of your weakness. So if your weakness is anger, you might not be getting mad at people and yelling at them but you still may be feeling irritable and impatient. Since I started working on myself my anger has gone down about 80%."

"It seems to take forever, doesn't it?" I asked.

"Transformation is a life journey. At the end you may not be 100% perfect, but you will be far better than those who haven't awakened and done anything for themselves."

My thoughts went to Michael and Claire as I heard Eric speak. Michael spoke of the role of 'kavanah', meaning intention, in spirituality. Without the right mindset, aka kavanah in Judaism, any attempt at spirituality is meaningless.

Then I thought of Claire chanting in the early days of her spiritual journey. And then I thought of how thirty years ago, when she was an artist living in New York and was hurting badly, having suffered the loss of many friends to AIDS, her personal loss had triggered deep transformation in her.

I am going to share with you a powerful experience Claire once shared with me because it beautifully describes how she relied on symbolism at a time when she underwent a deep awakening. The reason I am sharing this is because I really feel for people who get stuck in the spiritual add-ons, if I may use that word, and stop short of transforming the self. Over to Claire for her story -

"One day I felt the need to spend time on top of a sacred mountain in South Dakota (USA) called Bear Butte," she said. "On the way, I met a Native American man who listened patiently to my woes and advised me to give tobacco offerings to the earth as I climbed.

"'It will make your life better,' he said.

"I replied, 'I'm not an Indian and I don't want to play Indian and besides my life is pretty good'.

"The man looked at me meaningfully; I'd call it an aggressively passive look. I heard myself saying, 'Okay, okay, I'll do it'.

"As I climbed, I dropped little pinches of tobacco in thanks for every thing of beauty I encountered - the doves on the trail, the sound of wind in the pines and so on until I swear my heart was bursting with gratitude unconsciously stored up for years.

"I cried and I laughed. All fear and anxiety left me even though I had never done anything like this before. I felt loved, guided and protected and have ever since that night I spent on the mountain top, when I became a candidate for spiritual intelligence, when I was given a vision that continues to inform my life."

That night, Claire realized how much she had to be grateful for. She no longer had cause to complain. In her own words, "Ever since then, every morning, I sing a loving gratitude to the divine miracle of all and I listen and am inspired to help a confused world however I can."

She became aware that life and all creation is a miracle, an expression of the divine. She ended up packing up in New York and shifted to Bali, Indonesia, where she helps children. Since then, she has been better able to align her intentions with her behavior and her attitude.

It all started with her chanting but thank God it didn't stop there.

Lifestyle practices to increase your spiritual intelligence quotient

So you're reading this book. And maybe, just maybe, you are feeling inspired to think deeply about spirituality and apply it in your life. I'm delighted to hear so. May our tribe grow! May our enthusiasm never wane!

May I get in a word on enthusiasm? It is easy to feel enthusiastic about an initiative. The challenge is to sustain the feeling and hence, the effort. Sustaining any effort is essential because it takes time to learn any practice let alone make it work for you and those around you. I'm not saying to achieve perfection. Is there perfection in anything? After three decades of working on myself, I'm still a work in progress!

In the context of spirituality, practice is all the more essential because we live in an environment which is far from spiritual. Worldly affairs tend to deplete our energy, I am sure we all agree on that. Shivani Verma, the Raja Yoga meditation teacher who I call the bright star of the Brahma Kumaris for delivering talks around the world and for her global following (I first heard about her from a Canadian friend who used to watch her TV show!), gave me a great example to bring out this point.

"Suppose you live with three people," she said. "The first flies into a temper at the drop of a hat, the second worries about everything and the third takes stress from the simplest situation. Since you live with them, their vibrations will tend to rub off on you. If you are a sensitive person, as most of us have become, you may even experience your qualities change. You might feel yourself becoming an angrier person, a more worrisome person, a stressed out person.

"Is that how you want to feel?"

"No," I said.

"We all want to experience love, happiness and peace, don't we?" she said.

I nodded.

"So, how do we prepare ourselves to counter all the negative influences out there and charge ourselves in the process?"

"Meditation," I prompted.

She laughed.

"Yes. The spirit is like a battery which gets depleted because of negative influences. Just like a cellular handset which is so useful when it is charged, but stops working when it is discharged. I, the spirit, who has many roles and responsibilities to fulfil, must charge myself to stay strong."

"How long do you recommend meditating?"

"Meditating for half an hour at least is good."

You practice Raja Yoga meditation I know. Can you tell us what that involves?

"Raja Yoga meditation is based on the premise that God is the powerhouse. So we connect with God to absorb His power, feel His love, and heal emotional blockages."

"How can you tell if you have had a good meditation session?"

"I feel charged up. I feel I am radiating love, purity, bliss and power."

"What other practices can you recommend to sustain a spiritual endeavor?" I asked.

"You know what they say - we are what we read, watch and listen. I hear a spiritual lecture every morning. It helps remind me of my purpose in life."

I nodded because I have been privy to those lectures and have enjoyed them myself. "What exposure could you suggest for readers of my book?"

"I'd suggest avoiding reading newspapers and watching news channels the first thing in the morning. Instead, begin the day with thirty minutes of a healthy emotional diet of spiritual or self-transformation messages."

That sounded do-able. "What else?"

"During the day, I endeavor to exhibit my spiritual strength, that is, express love and reflect peace in my interactions with others."

"Essentially, you advocate a conscious attempt to stay spiritual?"

"Yes," she said.

In my own life my conscious attempt has been to not make the same mistake twice, which necessitates being aware of yourself and the people you interact with.

"What else," I prodded.

"I'm lucky that my profession, if you can call it so, involves sharing spiritual insights. Preparing for lectures ensures that I spend my time gainfully. It keeps me away from wasteful social talk about people."

I could relate to that. I was never any good at social chit-chat. I once dated a man who got so annoyed with me when I couldn't make polite conversation with his friends in a golf club. "Why can't you just talk about simple things?" he would ask. I always had the same answer, "because it is pointless". It always felt like a waste of energy.

I love to talk about what is happening in the world and about the condition of humanity. I love to learn and have always been curious and still am.

Shivani continued with one more tip to stay focused. "In the middle of everyday chaos, stop whatever you are doing after every fifty-nine minutes. For one minute, observe your thoughts. Create the shift from busy to easy, stress to relaxation, worry to confidence.

"Eating the right sort of food, which for me means food cooked in a meditative state, also helps stay on the spiritual path," she added.

"Yes," I agreed. I have dedicated an entire chapter to diet.

"Last but not the least, before going to sleep, spend a few minutes to resolve issues. Forgive anyone who has wronged you. Don't try to sleep on a negative thought."

"How long do you think someone would need to apply these changes before they begin to experience a positive effect?" I asked.

"I'd suggest experimenting with these tips for a month."

"How can someone tell if the changes are working? How can you tell if you are becoming more spiritually intelligent?" I was thinking of my friend Judy Buddle, who would also say you can't measure spiritual intelligence as you would measure ordinary intelligence, by taking an intelligence quotient test.

Shivani correlated spiritual intelligence with spiritual strength, and described a strong spirit as one that experiences happiness, peace and wisdom. A weak spirit experiences anger, stress, worry, jealousy.

So, what emotions are you experiencing?

Become the best version of yourself

In conversation with Nirwair, I learned more about his spiritual path.

"The first two things I was taught were 'know your real self' and 'have self respect'."

"How did those teachings make a difference to your life?" I asked.

"Knowing myself as a child of the Supreme, the greatest of great, the lord of lords, was very intoxicating. It stood out in stark contrast to the general perception of the self among devotees," he said.

"I don't quite understand," I said.

"God is held in high esteem in every religion," he explained. "But the popular belief among devotees is that their status is lowly, they are considered the dust of the feet of the Supreme. That means a child of the Supreme considers himself to be a particle of dust."

That sounded wrong to me. I shook my head.

"That is totally wrong," he endorsed.

I felt relieved.

"The path I chose awakened my self-esteem. I was taught to connect with the Supreme," he said.

"Do you mean meditation?"

"Yes, to connect with the Supreme through meditation. Raja Yoga meditation is a means to empower the self," he said.

I gathered that the idea was to draw on virtues, love, peace, happiness and any virtue you associate with the source of all good, during meditation, to become a better version of yourself.

I liked that. At the end of the day, of what use is spiritual intelligence if it doesn't help you become a better person? If we aspire to live in a better world, surely that starts with us?

This self-improvement thread came out strongly when I interviewed Kathy Barrett, my special friend living in upstate New York. During our conversation, she told me that she has always had an innate yearning to master the human condition.

"By that I mean I want to understand myself and always strive to be the best possible person I can be," she said.

And she went on to tell me how she is working towards that.

"I analyze every life experience as if I were a forensics detective solving a murder crime."

I chuckled.

"I look for clues that will show me what I could have done better and I look at where I failed and try to understand what led me to take this action and that action so I come away with a deeper understanding of myself, my wounds and the people around me. This raises the bar of awareness I strive to have in my life and despite my imperfections and failings the fact that I am in action trying to figure this all out brings me some peace of mind."

Kathy's analytical method was clearly very different to Nirwair's meditation practice to deepen his relationship with God but as I say, whatever works for you is good.

"That's great, Kathy," I said. "It's wonderful that you're conscious about becoming a better person. Can you give me an example of any time when your analytical mind helped you take a few steps in the right direction?"

Kathy proceeded to narrate an episode in her life.

"I had the opportunity to write someone's memoir. I believed in the person's story and felt that the world could benefit from the lessons she learned. I really believed it was my destiny to write this story but not for the reasons I originally thought," she said.

"Over four years, I lost my own identity while writing a story about a woman in search of hers. In completing this memoir, I ran myself into the ground. Working day and night adversely impacted my health. My relationships and my own projects suffered greatly. I willingly obliged requests that required me to do additional work outside the scope of the book and gave away even more time at great expense to myself and loved ones."

"You sound like you were senselessly driven," I said.

"Absolutely," she said "What I learned about myself in the process humbled me."

Kathy was lucky the mess she had created helped her realize her folly. "Were you comfortable with the person you saw yourself to be," I asked.

"Not at all," she said. "I realized that I had focused on work like a horse wearing blinders. In the process of realizing my ambition I had hurt my loved ones. Through the process of writing this memoir I saw aspects of my own character in the person I was working for which gave me clarity about who I had been in the past to other people. Deep down I struggled with not being or ever feeling enough. My ego was so fixated on getting to the finish line that my expectations and demands of others were unreasonable. I didn't appreciate or give other team members the credit they deserved for their contributions. This ME...ME...ME state of existence made me oblivious to reality and I completely lost sight of my original qualities."

I saw similarities between Kathy's awareness that when ego and insecurity define us we disconnect from our original qualities, which are positive, and Nirwair's description of meditation as a means to reconnect with the virtues we recognize in God, which we feel disconnected from.

Kathy said reflection has helped her concentrate her energies on feeling whole again, so today she is confident that fear and insecurity will never rule her again.

"I am able to recognize negative energies and prevent myself from falling down the same suffering well," she said.

"So now do you always feel in control?"

"No!" said Kathy. "What horrifies me is that despite my knowledge I still have bouts of what I call spiritual intelligence amnesia."

I gathered that there is never an end to becoming a better version of you.

"I have realized that there is always room for me to change and to improve," affirmed Sandra Slovenc Vojvodic.

Sandra is from Zagreb, Croatia. She is a businesswoman, family person and also the coordinator of the Raja Yoga meditation center in the city, which is how I got to meet her. I was passing through Zagreb, staying in a hotel but I wanted to connect with the person running Raja Yoga meditation courses in the city. Sandra graciously came to meet me in the hotel. My first impression of her was that she was a very beautiful, stylish young woman. When I got to know her better, what stood out was her clarity about where she has been and where she needs to go.

Chatting with her about becoming a better version of ourselves, she said spirituality has taught her that a mistake is a chance to refocus.

"Well, yes," I said. "It is important to not repeat mistakes."

"There is no reason why we should," she said. "We are living in a time when divine guidance is available to increase our spiritual intelligence quotient."

"Spiritual knowledge combined with the power of love discovered in meditation has shown me a more compassionate, kind, comforting and joyful side of life. Aren't we all in pursuit of constant happiness, joy and freedom, reminding us of our divine origin?"

Once again, a respondent put the focus on our lost divinity. It appears that the best measure of the quality of any spiritual pursuit is the extent to which we reflect divinity, virtues that the world is desperate for.

Use it (spiritual intelligence) or lose it

"If you don't put spiritual intelligence into practice, it is of no use, it is of no value."

Those wise words came from Dr Partap. When I interviewed him for this project, he made it clear at the outset of our conversation that theory didn't gel with him, and hence he made that opening comment about applying spiritual insights.

"Spiritual insights are valuable only when they become a part of you, of your life. That in turn will only happen when you relate spirituality to your life. If you cannot do so, the spiritual insight will be here today and gone tomorrow."

"That sounds like use it or lose it," I remarked.

"Precisely," he said. "That is how it works. And if you think of it, of what use is spirituality if it cannot help me control my life in a stressful situation, if it cannot give me self mastery? Life is very uncertain nowadays. Things change very fast. That makes spirituality absolutely essential."

Over the next twenty minutes Dr Partap gave me a few tips on applying spirituality to live better and work better, which I have summarized as follows:

Use silence and patience as tools

We all face difficult situations. Dr Partap recollected how he had moved from practicing medicine into management. "I never liked management but I got pushed into it," he said. "It was painful at first, particularly working in a public hospital with limited resources.

"You know, managers are meant to manage operations and troubleshoot problems. You need the right attitude to be an effective manager. But in my earlier days, I used to feel defensive when people came to me with their problems. Just seeing a sulking face could put me off. It took me many years to realize that my approach wasn't helpful to defuse the situation. Over time, I learned that I was meant to be a shock absorber. And that I needed to develop skills to help absorb shocks!"

I chuckled. "What were the skills you learned?"

"Silence, to start with. You need to learn to be silent. You also need to develop a lot of patience. Dadi Janki (the head of the Brahma Kumaris, Dr Partap is a long time practitioner of Raja Yoga meditation) says patience removes the pain in the mind.

"Also, you need to really listen to people, observe them. What are they trying to convey? Often, we react without listening. The ability to stay silent and patient can help listen."

Develop coping strategies

"So what do you do when you've had a rough day?" I asked.

"One of my coping strategies is to reconnect with my strongest experiences, moments when I felt spiritually strong," said Dr Partap. "When I am down, I remember those moments. It really helps.

"Another practice that always helps is the daily spiritual sermon that I read or hear in the morning," he added. "I draw a lot of strength and solace from those spiritual insights. It is my nourishment for the whole day."

Reduce your dependency on people

"We tend to easily accept that situations will be unpredictable. But one of my biggest learnings has been that people will be unpredictable," said Dr Partap. "Someone who is affectionate might suddenly become moody or turn away from you. I used to question why? Until I realized that everybody goes through their own stuff. Today I understand that you can't question why?

"Yes, it is important to have positive people around you. However, as far as possible, spiritually intelligent people will not depend on one or two friends for support. They will increasingly rely on themselves for a pick up. Ideally, your lifeline should be your solitude and your hobbies. Widen your canopy of solutions and let these come from you.

"Be independent in your thoughts and how you run your life. People can support you and guide you but you need to take your own decisions. You can't hold anyone responsible for your decisions."

Play to your strengths

One of Dr Partap's suggestions involved identifying your overriding virtues and leveraging those to your advantage.

"I am not highly intelligent but I have tried to make up by being sincere and being available in times of need," said Dr Partap. "When I practiced medicine, I really loved my patients. I really wanted to make their lives better. I learned to address them as people, not as patients. That helped me be a good doctor. Also, I learned to trust my intuition. Somehow, that helped me be available at the right time. I remember one time I was shopping. It was late evening. All of a sudden, I felt that I was needed in the hospital. I didn't ignore the feeling. I left what I was doing and headed straight to the hospital where I found a serious situation had arisen because of an altercation between two staff. My presence made a huge difference in sorting out the matter."

*

Here, I'd also like to share a method that Ken told me he uses to maintain his balance during tough times.

"First, I analyze things using my rational sensibility," he said. "Then I work on bringing up my feelings to the best possible level that they can be."

"What exactly do you mean by that? Do you mean you try to stay positive?" I asked.

"Yes. I invoke God's presence and ask 'how would you feel in this situation?' And I compare what I'm feeling with what I think He would be feeling and if it is different, I work on my emotions."

"Can you tell me how you adjust your emotions?"

"I ask myself what quality or virtue I need to be the personification of."

"Is it easy to identify what you need to be?" I asked.

"It requires honesty, a deep understanding of yourself and a strong connection with God."

"That sounds fascinating," I said. It really did. "It sounds like to bring out the best in you, you ask God to act as your consultant and you trust in him 100%, which is lovely," I said.

Ken smiled.

"If I have made Him my companion for life, I like to know what He must be feeling and if I'm not feeling the same, I need to ratchet up a couple of notches. So if there is a situation where I feel He would be an embodiment of peace and I am not, I practice being the way He is.

"You know, we sometimes fool ourselves into thinking that because we can understand something we have become it."

I nodded.

"But it doesn't work that way," he continued. "I don't just have to understand the whys and wherefores but make that information into wisdom. I have to be an embodiment of it."

*

Next up in this chapter on practicing spiritual intelligence is a story and an exercise, courtesy of David.

First, the story:

Gary Player, the top golfer was once in a bunker, a sand pit near the green or fairway that is purposely created as a hazard on a golf course. Now it is difficult to hit the ball out of the bunker but Gary chipped in two or three balls straight out of the bunker into the hole.

There was a guy watching him and he said, "Wow, Mr Player that was amazingly lucky. You got three balls in the hole."

Gary turned around and said "Do you know it's really funny, the more I practice, the luckier I get."

I chuckled and remarked, "Practice, practice, practice. What is your definition of practice?" I asked David.

"Practice is repetition. We have to repeat what is right," he said.

"What does that mean?" I asked.

"I'll give you another sporting example," David continued.

"I was once talking to a golf coach about grooving (following a drill), and I said, 'Well, practice makes perfect'.

"'Ah, ah, practice doesn't make perfect', he replied."

"'What do you mean?" I asked.

"'Perfect practice makes perfect', he clarified. Essentially, if you are repeating something that is imperfect, you are grooving something that is imperfect. So it has to be perfect practice."

"So if you practice something that is wrong then it is of no use," I said. That makes sense.

"Yes, you've got to practice perfectly again and again. It isn't as if you can wave a magic wand and become spiritually aware," said David. "Do you know, previously, spiritual intelligence was thought to be about knowing stuff. But it doesn't matter how much you know. You've got to apply it, perfectly."

"Hmm," I said. "In the context of spiritual intelligence, practice means becoming aware that I am a spirit and this body is a temporary costume. Is that correct?"

"Yes," said David. "And there is no need to make heavy weather of this practice Betty. It's really very simple."

When I didn't say anything - I was thinking about how many of my respondents, fairly spiritually evolved people had told me they struggled with meditation - David chipped in with an example.

"I was doing a course in meditation for a bunch of beginners and it just so happened that there was some repair work going on next to the venue. So you could hear a lot of clanging and banging."

"Not quite the right setting for meditation, huh?" I said.

"That is precisely what I was going to say," said David. "But you know what? I chose to use the noise to help my students focus."

"How did you do that?" I asked, genuinely curious.

"I said focus on the noise. Tell me what you can hear. Of course, they said they could hear clanging and banging."

"You don't need to make it go away, I advised. I want you to make a choice. Keep the noise there. Don't shut it out."

"Then," I prodded.

"Then I asked 'Who is listening to the noise?'"

"'What do you mean?' they asked."

"So I asked 'Who is aware that you would prefer it to be quiet?' That is when they started to see what I was getting at."

"'Are your ears listening to the noise?' I asked."

"'No', they said."

"'Is your brain listening to the noise?' I continued."

"'No', I prompted, 'because dead things don't think and the brain doesn't hear'."

I chuckled.

"It is you who is listening through this wonderful instrument, which has the brain and ears as part of its costume."

"It's easy to forget who we are," I remarked.

"Of course it is, because we are living through a body. That is why spirituality is a practice."

*

I'll sign off here with a thought from Pilar, my friend from Spain. Although spirituality is something new for most of us, she said, when you experience consciousness, call it pure life, it will seem as if you have always known it and therefore it will touch you deeply. You, the soul, will as though wake up from a sound slumber to this vital memory, buried deep within, and take on your role of caretaker of our planet.

PART SIX

Is self-evolution a lifelong process or is there a way of short circuiting it?

Back in 1990, I was really messed up. I had a big ego and I was running after things and relationships that weren't doing anything for me. Somewhere deep down I had the desire to change the way I lived. But I didn't know how to go about doing so. All I knew was that the need I was experiencing was important. It couldn't be ignored.

I started to meet up with people who I had heard had an interest in spirituality. Not that I could relate to the word spirituality. I had no clue what it means. As a step forward, I just wanted to do something to make my life better. I wanted to figure out life. Even that much wasn't easy.

My earliest experiences of meditation in my neighbor's house in Canada were terrifying. Silence unnerved me. Sitting alone scared me. I couldn't face my thoughts, something that both silence and sitting alone compelled me to do.

Some months later, I travelled to India, where there was so much more that upset me. I stayed in the Brahma Kumaris' world headquarters in Mount Abu. I had never met so many people who were consciously making an effort to meditate and who had a very different world view to mine (at the time). I couldn't make out if they were real or not. They felt pure, they looked pure, but I couldn't handle their purity.

When I stepped out of the campus, I saw poor people living in wretched conditions who were quite happy and I used to wonder why they seemed happy when there was no apparent reason for them to be happy.

A few years down the line, after a couple more visits to the Brahma Kumaris in India, it dawned on me that those poor people had figured out life. In all their poverty, they were far more peaceful and joyful than I had ever been in my wealth, so to speak. If something was good, it was good. If something wasn't good, it would be good, if not in their present life, then in their next life. Because they believed in reincarnation, they believed in eternal time, their source of happiness was not confined to the here and the now. Talk about being evolved!

It has taken me a lot of years to get to the point where I enjoy my own company and am comfortable with my thoughts. And can sort of take rude comments in my stride. And have some semblance of control on the way I respond to situations. And can say the word God without shaking (an emotional reaction I developed after experiencing intense anger toward Him after I lost my baby) - that happened about five years ago during a workshop on God being led by Jayanti. When I did say the G-word, she looked at me and said, "It only took thirty years."

I often wonder if it had to take me this long to reach where I am today. Is there no shortcut to experience the Ah-effect? Must self evolution be a lifelong process?

Samuel, my young philosopher friend in UK, reminded me that ancient Greek philosophers made the pursuit of truth their life's purpose, despite the fact that they knew that the process was hard work!

This process of figuring things out isn't a one-time thing. It is unending. It is a journey, said Sam.

"Essentially, we're trying to find our way home," he said.

Sam recollected St Augustine's concept of pilgrimage. When St Augustine referred to peregrinatio, a Latin word for leaving one's homeland and wandering for the love of God, he usually meant a journey to God or to heaven or a conversion or a better version of the self. St Augustine seldom meant a journey to an earthly holy place. Wandering to a holy mountain can help, but what we are actually looking for is bigger than the world.

Comparing self evolution to a journey made a lot of sense to me. I have traversed an amazing journey knowingly since 1990, and unknowingly since much before (starting with reading self help books during my teens), and crossed many interesting milestones along the way. Looking back, I can now see how events in my life unfolded and influenced me, and I can understand that the same situations would influence me differently now, or perhaps not influence me at all.

"So is it fair to say that we're trying to find the divine or God or whatever and become the best version of ourselves?" I said. It was a question more than a statement.

"Yes. And another important thing to realize is that this journey is not just a means to self evolution. It is also the goal," Sam continued. "If I could once again draw on philosophy to answer you, one point that philosophers make is that the most important things are not stepping stones to something else. Essentially, we want them for their own sake. Philosophers wanted this journey; they truly wanted to surrender their lives to something that matters. It was the only thing that really made them happy."

Sam's mentioning happiness in the same breath as the journey of self evolution really got me.

So if I were to consider this journey as an end in itself and not as a means for something else, I guess I'd never think of short circuiting it.

I felt very comfortable after this conversation. Even after all these years, I know I'm not quite there. Can we ever get to the best version of ourselves? Maybe. Maybe not. But Sam's suggesting that self evolution is a lifelong project meant that every day, no, every moment that I move forward, I have arrived. It really eased the pressure.

Do you need a guru?

In the West, there is some fascination with the idea of getting a guru, a mentor to guide you on the spiritual path. Some seekers even think of travelling to the East to find a guru.

When I chatted with Margaret, she referred to Jiddu Krishmurti, the well known mystic who many called their guru, nevertheless, who himself did not believe in the concept of a guru and didn't like to be looked upon as a teacher. He aimed at triggering a deep shift in people by getting them to think for themselves, to be their own champion, so to speak.

My own path started with a lot of reading. You could say I found my first guru in the written word, in particular, in books authored by the late Ram Dass, the American spiritual teacher, and former academic and clinical psychologist. He always made sense. As an aside, my favorite teaching from Ram Dass is his advice to treat everyone you meet like God in drag. Essentially, he meant everyone and everything we see are expressions of the divine, and as much as the outward form may not appeal to you, within the being is significance and beauty.

Some years later I started to sign up for retreats like Esalon in California that taught me vision painting and goal setting for my life. In Esalon, I met my friend Michael, someone I look upon as an early mentor for teaching me to be me.

Then during one of my early journeys, I met Claire, who I will always look upon as the person who taught me to take risks and enjoy the adventure, and always thank God. I would also call out my late friend Meredith Durham as a mentor. She had the amazing ability to calm me and get me to look at the bigger picture, to develop a vision for my life. It was too sad that she passed away far too young, in her fifties.

I was always very interested in conversations about life and would enjoy engaging with people who spent time in such reflection. One such opportunity stands out in my memory. It was in 1989 in Toronto, in the house of my then neighbor Anthony Phelips. Anthony was associated with the Brahma Kumaris. At that fateful meeting, I first met Dadi Janki, the present head of the group. When she held my hand when we were introduced, my body shook. I knew at that very moment that the (then) seventy-four year old lady in front of me was special.

In the years since, I have met Dadi every so often in different continents. I have come away richer from every meeting, with a new understanding of ego, humanity or humility. I love Dadi dearly and deeply admire her strength, her zest for life and her bluntness. Whenever I am asked if I have a spiritual mentor, I instantly think of Dadi.

A mentor is someone who is ahead of you on the spiritual path, and hence, who you can turn to when you are in need of a blessing. When I embarked on my travelling lifestyle at the age of seventy, I asked Dadi for her blessing and also for permission to visit certain centers of the Brahma Kumaris. She asked if I thought seventy was too old to start a travelling lifestyle. I said no. She just looked at me, waved her hand and said go. I took that as my blessing and permission!

Dadi was 103 years old when I met her last year to ask for her definition of spiritual intelligence. She sat in silence for two minutes. Seeing me start to get fidgety, her caregiver said, "Wait, she is thinking".

Dadi then took my hand, gave me a big smile and said, "Inner light".

Just two words but what depth they hold.

Dadi has always had 'tough' love for me. I say tough because she can be brutally honest. She's like that with the people she knows. She will shine a light to help you become aware of your weaknesses. When I chatted with Gopi, she remembered an incident that had happened when she was travelling with Dadi maybe close to two decades ago.

Gopi was travelling in the capacity of an assistant to Dadi, which meant that she was expected to do a number of things such as take notes for any inspirational message Dadi wanted to send out to students of Raja Yoga meditation or help her hand out gifts to the many people she met. It used to be joked that Dadi's energy levels were so high - even when she was in her late eighties, which is about how old she was in this incident - that she used to need a couple of assistants to get through the day. The assistants would tire of attending to Dadi but she would never get tired of service!

In the particular instance that Gopi remembered, it so happened that they were travelling from Mount Abu to the base of that hill town, a place called Taleti on the outskirts of Abu Road, where the Brahma Kumaris have this massive sixty acre campus called Shantivan. In those days it was quite normal for Dadi to address a gathering in the Brahma Kumaris' twenty-odd acre campus in Mount Abu and then travel about twenty-five kilometers down the winding hill road to address another gathering, and sometimes, travel back up to address a third audience! It's a beautiful drive but for someone with a weak stomach, the many twists and turns on the road are a challenge.

The incident that Gopi recollected happened on one such very busy day. Dadi was on form. Perched on the backseat, she didn't waste a single minute. To quote Gopi, "She was kind of sipping something, she was reading, she was on the mobile phone speaking to somebody. She put that down and continued reading."

You get the point. Dadi was on-the-go, non-stop.

As for Gopi, she was struggling with butterflies in her stomach and a giddy head. Leaning back in her seat, she hoped against hope that she wouldn't vomit in the car and create a scene.

Just then, without turning to Gopi, Dadi suddenly said, "Can you pull out your dictation pad? I want to dictate something to you".

Poor Gopi! The order came at a time when she couldn't even look up! It was all too much for her and she asked the driver to stop the car. He obeyed. Gopi got out quickly and started gasping for deep breaths in an attempt to control the nausea that was making its way up. Fortunately, the driver had some lemons (he must have been used to chauffeuring people with weak stomachs!) and handed her one, which helped calm her down and after a few minutes they resumed their journey.

"What was Dadi doing all that time that you were out of the car?" I asked Gopi.

"When I got back in, Dadi was still reading as if nothing had happened," she said.

I chuckled.

"Then she turned to look at me and pushed her glasses down the ridge of her nose and said, 'That shouldn't have happened to you,'" continued Gopi.

"And that was it for me. I put my hands together like a Namaste and said 'Any normal person would have asked me if I was okay, if I wanted a glass of water, and you say to me, this shouldn't happen to you'."

I laughed out loud. "What else did you say?"

"You're sixty years older than me, you're sipping, you're reading, you're talking in the car and nothing happens to you. Why does it happen to me?"

"Wow," I said.

"Yeah, it all just came out!" Gopi continued. "And then she started laughing at me."

I laughed too, thoroughly enjoying the story. "So, what did she say? You must have got a sermon."

"She said 'You people waste your time, energy and breath in small ways'. And she asked me what I was doing at lunch time? Then she said 'Dadi was eating in silence remembering Baba (God). What were you doing? You were gossiping with another sister'."

"Wow, what did you say?" I asked.

"I accepted what she had said. It was true. She went on to explain that when you waste your time, thoughts and energy, the wastage builds up as a burden in the soul and that burden affects the balance of the body, causing the sort of suffering I was experiencing."

"Straight talk, huh?" I said.

"It was like a bullet from a gun but she gave me what I needed. That is her love," Gopi said. "Someone could have patted my back and cared for me, but I didn't really need that. I needed the love that liberated me from my condition."

"She is an amazing person," I said.

"One thing I have always appreciated about Dadi is that even though she is my mentor, she has never acted like a mentor," said Gopi. "She's actually only just ever been my friend."

"That's lovely," I said.

"She has respected me deeply as a friend and she has been a very truthful friend. She has been my ultimate ego killer. She has helped me see parts of myself that I can't see or see myself when I'm acting under a negative influence. Her love and mercy came from a space of deep truth. And that is so important because I think on a spiritual journey you do need good friends and good friends give you feedback."

*

Looking back on my life journey, I don't think you can walk the spiritual path by yourself. Finding a group of like-minded people gives you the support you need to keep your spiritual interest alive, and it helps ensure conversations start from the same place. In the last three decades I have developed deep friendships with many people practicing Raja Yoga meditation taught by the Brahma

Kumaris. I have learned from all of those associations. Having said that, I have also picked up spiritual insights from many friends who have never been associated with any formal spiritual group, many of who I interviewed for this book, which just goes to show how important it is to stay open to learning.

I also feel that as time moves on and you narrow down the virtues that are important to your own path, you need to go on your own. Basically you need to become your own person and develop your own relationship with God and yourself. This will necessitate you to spend time in silence, in contemplation.

The question, 'to belong or not to belong (to a group)' - which I think is very similar to, 'to find or not to find a guru', because arguably, every group is headed by a guru and every guru is associated with a group, also raises questions over the quality of the institution you choose to associate with.

An organization may be founded to promote a spiritual path, and in time, its messaging could get diluted, or the collective focus of followers on the mystical practice could wane. So when you get too involved with an institution, there is always the possibility that you stray from spirituality.

Discontentment with institutions is a real concern in our world. Will observed that from the 1960s onwards there has been a general disillusionment in institutions at all levels, in their authority, in their integrity, in our trust in them and in their viability.

"If you look around you, you will see that many institutions in North America and Europe have failed," said Will.

"So do you see a role for institutions in spirituality?" I asked.

Will made it clear that institutions play a big role in social change because it is through institutions that we are able to organize on a larger scale and for the longer term beyond the individual initiative or charismatic impact of a particular person. He attributed the failure of institutions to the lack of leadership at all levels of society and around the world.

For me, Will's observation takes the discussion back to the level of the individual. Can I think for myself? Can I lead myself? Can I sustain myself? It comes down to taking responsibility for me, to developing my inner light.

What do spiritually intelligent people eat?

When I interviewed Neville he shared an interesting anecdote about his experience with vegetarianism. Incidentally, he has been a vegetarian for thirty-seven years.

In the early days when Neville started to meditate, one day, his meditation teacher pointed out that since he was enjoying the practice and having good experiences, he might want to try a vegetarian diet.

"She said 'Your meditation will be better if you follow a vegetarian diet'," recounted Neville.

"So were you a non vegetarian then?" I asked.

"Oh yes, I didn't have any sense of the ethical elements of diet at that point in time. That was before I started to read about industrialized agriculture and the ill treatment of animals. I just ate meat unthinkingly."

I nodded.

"I was experimenting with my diet a fair bit in those days," he continued. If I was going out with friends for dinner and they ordered something that had meat in it, I would eat it out of politeness. However, for a few days after that, I would experience something like a curtain on my awareness."

"Ah!" I said.

"It wasn't as if I dropped dead or anything," said Neville. "But it was just that my awareness seemed fuzzy."

"And obviously, that impacted your meditation," I asked.

"Of course," said Neville. "Later on, when I started to consciously stick to a vegetarian diet, I felt it gave me an immediate return in terms of the quality and depth of my meditation experiences."

"I think adjusting your diet is something you can do very quickly and fairly straightforwardly depending on your circumstances, and reap great returns," he added.

I can second what Neville said. Although, I must admit, vegetarianism as a concept has appealed to me more from the perspective of being healthy than for ethical reasons.

I have never had great affection for animals. That is why a few years ago, during the early years of my nomadic lifestyle, I signed up for a unique experience in Mauritius. It was called 'walk with lions' and as the name suggests, it was an opportunity for participants to walk alongside two lions.

'Walk with lions' was a new initiative. I saw it as an once-in-a-lifetime adventure. Also, somewhere deep inside, I felt that respect for nature was an element of spirituality that I needed to work on. Perhaps this opportunity to experience animals up close would nudge me forward in that area.

The walk would last one hour and the path would pass through a jungle. I would be accompanied by one guard armed with a gun and a knife, and a lion trainer carrying food. It sounded interesting!

I was advised to wear simple light-colored clothes, nothing loud, no patterns and no prints. I stuck to blue jeans and a white long-sleeved T-shirt.

I was also made to fill out a consent form and put through an interview during which I was asked questions such as how I dealt with quietness and so on. It was all a little strange but I understood where they were coming from. They were being extra careful, making sure I wouldn't freak out. I was happy with that!

Just before starting out, I was told to walk alongside the lions but to make sure I was a step behind their heads. I was given a stick and told to use it if either or both of the lions made a sudden move toward me, in which case I was to hold the stick between the lion and me. Talk about nerve wracking. I quivered from head to toe.

As we started down the path the trainer gave both the lions a big piece of raw meat each.

One of the first things to hit me as we walked was how large, long, tall (about as tall as my neck), sleek, heavy and powerful lions are. I felt very small and insignificant in their presence. Not for nothing are lions called the king of the jungle.

We walked in silence. All you could hear was the rustle of leaves on trees and under our feet/paws. Every so often, one of the lions would turn its head and look at me.

"Smile," commanded the trainer. "Don't look scared or angry."

I smiled obediently.

Lions have a long stride but they move very slowly. I gave over myself to the two lions and moved at their pace. I felt as if they were commanding me to respect them by the way they held themselves and looked at me, and the beauty is I did.

At the end of the hour, after I moved away from the lions, I felt a sense of relief. Only then did I realize how tensed up I had been.

From Mauritius I travelled to the Democratic Republic of Congo to hopefully scratch one item off my bucket list - my desire to see silver-back gorillas up close.

I stayed with friends in Goma, from where we started out one morning for a spot where a guard and guide were waiting for me. From there on we travelled in a jeep with two guards and an assortment of guns because we were driving through rebel territory. Along the road I saw many armed men wearing face masks. It was just like I had seen on CNN news. I was very scared but I have learned to let go and trust. The situation reminded me of an incident from many years ago. I was in Vietnam, boarding an Air Vietnam plane, an ancient, Russian built aircraft that didn't have any seat belts. As it taxied down the runway with no belt to keep me firmly in my seat, I wondered if the pilot was equally ancient or knew what to do. I remember saying to myself, 'The pilot doesn't want to die'!

In Congo, I thought, 'The guards must know where they are taking me'.

Many hours later having driven over rough roads we reached a lovely hotel where I would stay the night before leaving to see the gorillas in the morning.

A helicopter parked on the front lawn told me that some VVVIP must also have checked in. I found out it was Warren Buffet's son Howard. Apparently, he was there to check on projects his family foundation had funded, which involved providing equipment and covering the salaries of the park rangers employed to protect the wildlife.

Two guides, two guards and I set out in the morning. I had no clue how far we would have to trek to reach the gorillas. Well, it took us two solid hours of rough walking just to reach the fringe of the jungle. After that, as we had to make our way through dense underbrush, the going became much tougher. Tougher for me, I mean. It seemed to be a piece of cake for my protectors. In fact, the guides walked ahead of us, cutting up the underbrush to make it easier for me to pass. At one point we had to climb a steep slope. It was very slippery as it had been raining. Seeing me struggle, one of the guards scooped me on his back and carried me up. Honestly, if he hadn't done that I would have had to get down on all fours to climb up.

Gorillas move from spot to spot every day. One of the guides had a tracking device to identify their current location. It was in a clearing we were nearing. I was exhausted but dying to see what I had come all this way for.

I was asked to wear a face mask before moving closer. Silverback gorillas have no immunity. They catch everything, which is why you can't see them in a zoo.

A few steps ahead, there they were. Twenty six silver-back gorillas. A family. A father, several mothers, lots of children and some babies.

The father seemed content to lie on his back, brushing off flies. The mothers were busy grooming their children, brushing their hair with their fingers or picking berries off the trees to feed their young. The little ones were jumping and playing all over the place. One was in the tree next to me.

I was in awe. It was unbelievable. I had never seen anything like it before. They were like a human family. Caring and loving one another. Every so often they turned to look at me but didn't seem to be too concerned at all. I felt very privileged to be there, experiencing the stillness of the jungle and the beauty of those creatures.

We spent two hours with the gorillas. The hours flew by. When the guard signaled to me that it was time to leave, I became aware of tears in my eyes. I just couldn't believe what I had been part of.

But guess what? It was the same distance back. There were no shortcuts, no pick-up points and we had to hurry to get back before dark because it was unsafe to be out in those parts after sunset. We made it just in time. I was filthy dirty, covered in mud, but I felt so fulfilled. No description in a travel brochure would match that experience, as tough as it was.

The true value of those two experiences in expanding my horizon sank in, in the weeks after.

I thought a lot about those lions and the silver-back gorilla family. I realized that it is impossible to eat meat if you have understood that animals have personalities and emotions. Animals are individuals in their own right and they develop just as strong relationships and bonds between each other as do humans. Sure, I spent time with lions and silver-back gorillas, which are by no means animals we think of or consume as food, nevertheless, every animal is worthy of respect, cattle and goats just as much as wildlife.

I'd like to end this chapter by narrating something Jenny said when I interviewed her for this book.

Jenny recollected a talk by Christopher Herbert, the former bishop of St Albans (in the UK), to the staff of a charity for older people. "He introduced them to talking about spirituality by thinking of times and places that had a very special meaning for them, essentially situations that took them beyond the mundane into a realm that is not affected by everyday considerations," she said.

I leaned in to listen carefully.

"His premise was daily life tends to be very consuming, what with working, looking after others, shopping and so on."

I nodded.

"His idea was to help people go beyond their daily life, and in doing so, help them become aware of themselves and connect with their inner being."

"What did people say?" I asked.

"People responded with all sorts of things. Some spoke of a beautiful scene in the countryside. Some recollected a scene from their childhood. Others spoke of an emotion they felt when with another person or even when with a beloved animal."

Ah! I thought. I could relate to the latter, and I shared my experience with the lions and silver-backs with Jenny.

She smiled.

"I understand. I have felt intensely spiritual when I have spent time with animals," she said. "Activities that are sometimes talked about as creating flow can help experience spirituality."

"Does flow mean being fully involved in the moment and understanding that it is just one moment in time?" I asked.

"It is more about experiencing being outside time. Any sort of creativity can do that, can't it? Painting, music, even walking up a hill and as I said, spending time with an animal has contributed to my emotional health."

Mine too, I thought.

How can practicing detachment help you stay positive when you face adversity?

As I write this, an old friend is close to death. We go back decades.

My accountant who has been with me for thirty-five years had surgery for a critical condition yesterday.

I've sent them love and best wishes. I've let them know I am available but I've taken care to ensure that I don't come across as intrusive.

If this had been me a decade ago, I would have called them often, been on top of them asking how they are and what I can do to help. I love to help people but there have been umpteen times when people have seen my offer to help as interference.

What's changed?

I have. I have learned detachment. I have learned that my offers to help were my own ego talking; they had nothing to do with my friends. I have learned to be there for people but not in a pushy way. I've learned that you can be lovingly involved without being in your face. I have learned to let go. And that is good.

To be detached does not mean to not care. It means, when you hear or see something sad, you don't get carried away by your emotions because you understand what is going on. Or, as my friend Savi said, you don't reflect the same negative emotion that is being expressed by the afflicted person.

Say someone is crying. And you go up to them and start crying too. You'd be said to be resonating the same emotion.

"Of what use would you be to someone who is sad if you just share their sorrow?" said Savi. "Typically, when we hear something adverse, we respond with the same emotion that the other person is expressing. We just jump into the same thing."

Instead, Savi suggested, "If we could use an appropriate virtue, if we could embrace sorrow with love and strength and power, we could help the person to internally transform their sorrow."

"Do you think we can take away sorrow?" I asked.

"No, you can't take away sorrow but you can dull it with love so that the sorrow gets kind of suffocated and takes a backseat.

"We tend to respond to sadness with words and actions. But there is very little you can do to alleviate sorrow with words and actions," Savi added. "We need to go beyond these limits. Virtues are far more powerful. But to express positive emotions and bring about a positive change, you need to experience inner silence. You need to de-clutter the mind from what is going on around you."

Savi's words got me thinking.

I used to think when people are sad you should just be a good listener and show support to them. I didn't think that you can spread happiness. I thought people take time to get over sadness. That in due course, they begin to notice little things that will bring the feeling of happiness, may be a sunny day, the singing of birds, flowers, seeing friends, children playing, etc.

To become a good listener, I learned detachment. I learned how to manage my own emotions. I got into the habit of sitting in a quiet place - so much better if there is a water body nearby, a lake or ocean or stream always calm me - and practiced allowing my rational sense to take over the issue. Essentially, that involved keeping my emotions aside and figuring out what I need to do.

The interesting thing is you can apply detachment to every facet of your life to really feel free. In letting go of fixed ideas you give yourself a gift to explore, to be curious and non-judgmental and accepting of new ideas, thoughts and truths.

Practicing detachment has helped me to stay neutral and positive in the face of adversity. It has helped me manage my relationship with my children Jody and Julie, who I love very much but with whom I have had a very troubled bond since I decided to walk out of a bad marriage. They were in their teens at the time. I chose to let them stay with my ex-husband because it eliminated a custody battle. I didn't want to drag them to court when I was so messed up myself. Larry (my ex) was also financially better off and (I thought) that would make life easier for them. Honestly, if I hadn't gotten divorced, I would have lost my mind. After I walked out, I saw Jody and Julie a few times a week and they would come over to my apartment for meals. But for the most part they had to manage themselves until Larry remarried.

It seems to me that I have been paying the price for not playing the conventional role of a mother and wife ever since. My relationship with Jody has always been difficult, which is a pity. With Julie, my relationship fluctuates from very good, when we are like friends and sisters, to good, bad and very bad. I feel sorry about this situation and somewhere within, no matter whether they acknowledge it or not, I know they must feel some sadness too.

When I chatted with Elisabeth, I found she too had needed to learn detachment to negotiate her family life.

"I sometimes get the feeling that I have not brought up my children as well as I should have," she said.

"What do you mean?" I asked.

"Well, they are good people but they have little interest in spirituality and in going to Church. I always felt that the Church had a place for me. But my son doesn't want to experience that. I wanted my son to expose his children more to the Church but he was not interested in confirmation. I feel sorry about that."

"Tell me about it," I said. I often hope my grandchildren will retain some of their culture as they grow.

Using detachment to deal with children came up in my conversation with Mathilde as well. I asked her what she wanted for herself in the sense of what she still felt she had to learn.

"I don't want to have any more waste thoughts about anything happening around me or about anyone," she said, before giving me some context of that thought. "My son and daughter-in-law and grandchildren came to live with me a few months ago and occasionally, my old missionary habit of wanting to change people emerges. They are always online, in another world, you know how it is."

I nodded.

"I want them to be like we were when we grew up, eating together, spending time together. Forget it. I keep reminding myself to let go that it should be done like this."

"It's called detachment," I said.

"I know. How long does it take to learn," said Mathilde.

We both had a good laugh.

Detachment has allowed me to respond better in tricky situations and protect myself from feeling upset. It is an unending practice. Sometimes, things happen and I feel sad. Then I remind myself to let go. Sometimes, I can maintain my distance and not feel sad at all, or very little. A lot depends on the situation. You win some, you lose some. Gradually, you get better at winning.

Detachment is the only way to stay happy. From Savi, I learned that it is also a powerful means to spread happiness.

What can you learn from suffering?

Not so long ago, I watched the video footage of a crowd standing in front of the burning Notre Dame in Paris, singing Ave Maria. The gesture was touching.

But I wondered as I often do when I see an outpouring of grief after a horrific event, a classical example being the outburst of rage after every school shooting episode in the US, why does the emotion subside so soon? Before you know it, people get on with their lives, they move on.

Sure, the story is different for those who are directly impacted. They grieve, they mourn and occasionally, they grow.

"My toughest life experiences have been my biggest learning experiences," said Manuela Stoerzer, a special friend. Manuela is hip, she is beautiful, and that is why she is a model. She is also a life coach. She describes herself as Europe's first walking coach.

"I agree with you," I said. My deepest moments of introspection and growth have followed some of the most tragic instances of my life, such as losing a baby, getting a divorce and losing a loved one.

I think suffering compelled me to question, to make sense of life.

Manuela attributed the growth that comes out of suffering to the concept, the way of suffering.

In the book The Way of Suffering, Jerome Miller examines a fundamental claim of our culture, that suffering is the greatest spiritual teacher. Crisis challenges our effort to stay in control of our lives, according to him. In a crisis situation, all our illusions about control are stripped away and we are forced to face the harshest reality of all - even our existence is not something we can claim as our own.

Essentially, crisis, whether the loss of a loved one or the failure of a project you poured your heart into, creates emptiness. It brings us a step (or two or three) closer to experiencing death, the ultimate loss of the sense of self.

In taking away our sense of control over life, suffering prompts questioning to find out what is real; it prompts a journey to the truth. Suffering can open a mind. It can create a desire to go beyond the mundane. Many of those who are deeply touched by suffering find that life can never be the same.

To quote Miller, 'The way to find our heart is to return to our most haunting moments, those times when all the things we have kept hidden from ourselves seem on the verge of breaking through our long, laborious avoidance of them.

'Suffering has a way of turning everything upside down. And from that overturned perspective, it makes no sense to resume one's ordinary life - because one knows now the truths it was designed to keep hidden.'

The truth that we uncover during suffering varies. Different situations bring different learning.

For Glynis, parting ways with her husband brought her the gift of forgiveness.

Here's her story -

"When I discovered that it was him and my friend, I was devastated.

It came as a shock. My whole belief system was massacred. I had believed that we were together forever...

"People around me sympathized with me. They said the usual: 'What a bastard! What a bitch!'

"One exception was a colleague. Six to eight months down the line, one day she turned around and said to me, 'You know you'd be better off forgiving the other woman. Because like it or not, it's what you're going to find yourself doing. You will have to do it at some point and I'd recommend that you do it sooner.'

"That came as a surprise. Nobody was talking about forgiveness at that point. Conversations about my situation were always very vindictive.

"But that colleague of mine had the nerve, the courage to make an out-of-the-box suggestion. You've got to do it woman, she urged.

"She insisted that I look at myself rather than constantly look at other people.

"I started to think about what he had done. It wasn't good. But might I have been at fault too?

"One of my sisters said something that strengthened my questioning narrative. 'Well, I don't blame him for leaving you,' she said. 'You're a stroppy bitch.'

"I hated her at the moment but she was right. If people had focused on how I was, they would have thought, I don't blame the guy.

"I realized that the reasons why he did whatever he did, did not merit locking him up and throwing away the key forever.

"I chose to turn away from the greater narrative, 'Oh what a bastard, how dare he? Oh what a bitch, how could she, she was your friend.'

"I chose to learn from the divorce.

"I accepted the gift of forgiveness.

"I had to forgive him. But in forgiving him, the first person I had to forgive was me."

"Just remember that when you hit the bottom you have to come up," said Manuela. "Give yourself a chance to heal; that is most important."

Manuela recollected when she was about six or seven, a young man touched her inappropriately. Confused and hurt, she didn't tell her parents.

"I cried and cried, but I didn't tell anyone. I felt depressed for days afterwards. I felt worthless and I felt that worthlessness would last my entire life. To me, the situation was irrevocable. I was ruined for life."

A month or two later, her father committed suicide but the young Manuela was told that he had suffered a heart attack.

"I had a vague idea that it was something more sinister. Either way, it was a second blow to my shattered being."

Manuela did not face her demons just then. Life moved on.

A few years ago Manuela visited Ayahuasca, a Shaman healing retreat in Peru.

There, she was compelled to face her memories from long ago.

"I broke down once again but in this facing of grief, I felt I got back my dignity," she said. "It often happens when you push away stuff from the past, when you bury it, it doesn't get the air it needs to heal, just like a wound needs air. Give yourself a chance to heal and grow," she reiterated.

"What tips would you give to someone who wanted to overcome something negative?" I asked.

"Become aware of your thoughts and emotions, first of all, allow yourself to feel hurt all over again and then figure out what is real and what is a trigger," she said.

"What is a trigger?"

"Anything someone says or does that causes you to react," Manuela explained. "When something is being triggered it means something needs to be healed. Until you get to that point, consider any negative feeling that emerges as an opportunity to learn."

"How would you advise people to go beyond reacting?" I asked.

"It helps if you can remember that bad stuff is made of the same energy as good. If you can change your outlook, you don't need to call bad stuff suffering and you can harness energy to heal and grow," she said.

"That's a deep statement," I said.

"Life is all about duality, isn't it?" she said. "This is the game we play on earth. So much depends on how we choose to look at things. A sunflower always tries to turn toward the sun. I believe it is Nature's law to strive for happiness and wellbeing after feeling pain."

Take charge of your life

Social responsibility is a great virtue and the need of the hour. But, can it be cultivated, and if so, how?

Here, I'd like to bring in my interaction with Gopi. Her biggest contribution to my churning on spiritual intelligence was her simple yet powerful examples of taking responsibility for the self, which is arguably, the first step towards taking responsibility for the world. If you can't be responsible for yourself, you most certainly can't be responsible for the world.

Gopi described spiritual intelligence as knowing your role in the world, knowing God's role and knowing the role of others. "Step one is to know your path, understand it, claim it and take responsibility for it," she said.

"That sounds great, Gopi," I said. "But can you give me a practical example of what you mean by living more responsibly? Also, how would you advise someone to live more responsibly?"

"Okay, so let's consider health since health consciousness is on the rise nowadays. We all want to be healthy. To be responsible for my health means working out what I need to do to get healthy. It involves working out my lifestyle, working out my diet, working out my exercise and working out my attitudes.

"All of that requires a lot of focused effort and attention. Do you agree?"

"Of course," I said.

"Good. But you know what, look around you, how many people do you see making that effort?"

"I guess not many."

"You're right. In general, Betty, people are tired. They would rather stay dependent on a system - the medical system, which prescribes you pills for all sorts of diseases - because it is easier, even if it means that they then go on to blame everyone else for feeling the way they feel, if and when the pill doesn't work.

"The thing is, by not taking responsibility for yourself, you are perpetuating a culture of blame, you are constantly giving away your power and your self esteem to other people."

"True," I said. "But as you rightly said, people tend to take the easy way out. Do you think we have been conditioned to look for the easy way?"

"Well sure," said Gopi. "The system we live in promotes interdependence, partly because of money. You know, companies develop medicines that are supposed to make us better, and they do work, but they can also have side effects."

"In that scenario what does a spiritually intelligent person do?

"You've got to observe the effect of drugs on your body and when you know that that something isn't working for you, stop."

"So what you're saying is we need to get aware to be responsible?"

"Yes. To increase your awareness is also an act of responsibility. When you start to observe what is going on, you can start to get informed about things, you can start to make choices for yourself."

"That's interesting," I said. "Because I think we often react without thinking things through or as you would probably say, without observing."

"That's because people tend to think that observing means doing nothing," said Gopi. "That it is a passive path. That isn't correct. A spiritually intelligent person is not passive. He or she is proactive in the field of life, in the field of action. If you don't even observe what is happening, then it is like your whole mindset has bought into an interdependent system that dictates a certain life pattern, and you can't think beyond it. So you end up thinking this is how life is, this is how it will always be, and we have to be like this. No, actually you don't."

I really liked what Gopi said. I must confess I've always felt uncomfortable around whiners. I have great belief in our ability to make things happen. But I wanted to go a little deeper in to the subject of taking responsibility.

"Gopi, health is a physical aspect of life," I said. "Taking responsibility for our emotional wellbeing is somewhat more challenging, wouldn't you say?"

"I think when we cultivate self awareness then we gain access to resources that we never knew existed, which can help us rise to bigger challenges," she said. "I'll give you an example."

"I was fourteen when my family relocated to England from Africa. My brother and I were enrolled in a school where we were the only two Asians.

"I was young and quite naïve at the time. I had no idea racism exists. I had no language for racial discrimination but I faced a fair amount of it. Most of it took on the form of exclusion but there was a time it crossed a line. In particular, three people decided to take it upon themselves to give me a hard time.

"I couldn't understand why they used to pick on me. It was hard. I would go home crying everyday and wonder why I was facing what I was?

"I remember one time I walked into a classroom. Those three entered after me and locked the door. They pinned me to a desk and took an ink pad and rubbed ink on my whole face. There I was, lying on the desk feeling very helpless wondering 'What are you guys doing?'

"I was hurt. I was crying. I remember walking home and not wanting to go back to school ever again."

"Then," I prompted.

"Strangely, I felt protected even in my worst moments. I thought about what was happening but I didn't understand why they were doing what they were doing. Then I thought, maybe they don't understand why they are doing what they are doing as well. So I decided to go to the meditation center that was just next to my school every morning (Gopi learned how to meditate at the age of eight and has been meditating ever since) and send them a lot of good wishes.

"So for the next one month I had good wishes for those three. While I was meditating I would feel I was receiving so much love from God and have incredibly good wishes for them from my heart. I hope you wake up feeling good today. I hope you have a nice day."

I was sitting at the edge of my seat with bated breath, very curious to know what had happened next.

"Six weeks later those three people had turned around so radically in their attitude towards me that they became my best friends."

"Wow. Do you think that happened because you meditated?"

"I put it down to the incredible energy that became available to me when I meditated with God. Sometimes we can't access our good wishes by ourselves. However, a spiritually intelligent person knows how to take help from God. A spiritually intelligent person will answer the call to become a creator of his or her own life, with God's help. Cultivating a pure attitude will transform attitudes."

I was on another tangent by then. I asked Gopi if the three perpetrators, so to speak, had apologized to her.

"One of them apologized. But you know what, by that time it didn't matter to me."

"Why?" I asked.

"Well, because we are responsible for our karma. I decided to be responsible for my karma. I decided to be proactive about how I felt, rather than fall back into a blame mode. Far from feeling victimized, I felt so victorious because I had changed my energy. I didn't need to forgive anyone. In fact, I don't even believe you can forgive anyone, in the sense of releasing another person from their karmic accounts. We all need to settle our score. If you do wrong, you reap something that is not nice."

I thought Gopi's stories made great examples of how we can take control over our own lives and steer ourselves in the right direction.

Another of my interviewees (and friends) has made it her life mission to encourage people to create their own life, and that implies being responsible for yourself. Manuela specializes in opening up minds, transforming mindsets and changing habits by asking inspiring, uncomfortable and dangerous questions. For those reasons she counts herself in the small group of people who wouldn't ever get depressed! Why small? Over to her for that explanation:

"My sister once gave me a book on happiness. It included studies on depression! It suggested that 50% people will develop depression because of their genes and 40% because of their upbringing. So you're left with just 10% of people who will create their own destiny."

"And you're in that 10% group?" I asked.

"Yes, I'm in that group," said Manuela. "I'm not a revolutionary but I am of the firm opinion that you can find reasons to not be sad. You don't have to perpetuate the negativity that has been inflicted on you."

"Well, depression does sometimes creep up on us because of stuff we go through in the world," I said.

"Yes, some people blame the bad condition of the world for the way we show up in the world," said Manuela. "All those emotions are in the mind. Our monkey mind makes us feel that way. But you can't trust what is going on in your mind because it is influenced by your genes and your upbringing."

"And that is why you help people to open up their mind?"

"Yes, you are not a product or a victim of your parents or of your upbringing. We need freedom from such bad excuses. We need to use our free will to make responsible decisions. God helps those who help themselves."

Spirituality does not mean ignoring your physical needs

In his interview Nirwair acknowledged the need to combine spiritual consciousness with care of the physical being.

"Care of the physical being and the physical surroundings are very essential to help a person remain in higher consciousness," he said.

I really appreciated that statement because I have never been able to identify with the image of an unwashed, unkempt yogi (person who meditates). If you need a simile, think of images of hippies smoking pot bunched around an Indian guru with flowing locks that never seem to have been washed.

Balance.

I like the concept. The way I see it, if you don't pay attention to every facet of your life, you can't be a whole person. You cannot profess to be fully in control of your mind if you have an unhealthy body.

Taking my vitamins, getting some exercise and spending time outdoors (especially near water because it is very restful) are as much a part of my life as are meditating and being there for my grandchildren and friends.

I interviewed quite a few people in Mount Abu for this book. One of those was Binny Sareen, a unique person for having spent almost all her life in the hill town.

Binny's parents decided to relocate to Mount Abu from North India after being influenced by the spiritual knowledge of the Brahma Kumaris. Binny - and her brother and sister - grew up in the midst of senior sisters and brothers who were practicing Raja Yoga meditation. I was curious to know if someone with that background would also value balance in life, and how she found her equilibrium.

"So Binny," I said. "How old were you when you moved to Mount Abu?"

"I was six years old."

"When did you get to know about the Brahma Kumaris?"

"My parents explained the meaning of soul and spirituality soon after we relocated. They taught me how to meditate."

"Did you enjoy meditation at that age?"

"Yes. I liked it. I spent a lot of my time in the headquarters of the Brahma Kumaris."

"So you were brought up knowing the soul and I presume you could identify with yourself as a spirit," I said.

"Yes."

I have been to Binny's place several times for high tea, especially during visits to Mount Abu to volunteer at the J Watumull Global Hospital & Research Center, a healthcare initiative of the Brahma Kumaris. Having grown up in Mount Abu, Binny was very helpful in introducing me to the who's who of the town. Her parents, who have now passed away, were very gracious and charming. Binny's father was ninety-three and still going to their store when he passed.

"Binny, I remember one of the first times I came over to your place for tea, you recounted having Dadi Prakashmani, then the administrative head of the Brahma Kumaris and Brother Nirwair, managing trustee of the Global Hospital & Research Center over for dinner. Were you in awe of them?"

"I respected the seniors but I wasn't in awe of them probably because I grew up in their midst. The guidance I received from those senior members of the Brahma Kumaris has inspired me all my life."

"Growing up in such close proximity to people who were so spiritual, was it challenging to find your balance?"

Binny smiled. "I thank my mother for that," she said, and went on to explain. "I schooled in Mount Abu. Abu had no college in those days, and so, many youth from the town didn't get a higher education. Many of my own friends also did not study beyond school. Some seniors dissuaded me from studying further, saying I didn't need an education to serve the world. However, my mother took a very strong stand. She insisted that I study further. She told me that a higher education would help me in life and it would even enrich my spiritual life. I was a bright student. I went on to get a graduate degree and a few years ago, you know I was awarded a doctorate in spirituality. Most people around me dissuaded me from getting a doctoral degree but my family was supportive."

I knew about Binny's doctoral project. I think I was the first person outside the university to see her thesis. It is a massive tome, and I mean massive.

"I think it was great that your mother steered you in the right direction, I said. So it isn't as if you ever got put off spirituality because you had so much of it around you?"

"No, no. I ended up doing a doctorate in spirituality! In fact, I used to sit in the meditation room in the headquarters of the Brahma Kumaris to write my thesis and I had very deep spiritual experiences during that time. I felt God was helping me."

"So if you had to pinpoint a couple of learnings from your exposure to spirituality that you value the most, which would they be?"

"One practice I picked up from the seniors is to see the qualities of others no matter who the person is. When you make a conscious effort to see the good in others, you naturally come closer to people. It helps understand each other. It helps build relationships."

"That is a beautiful learning."

"I also learned to be patient when dealing with people who are confused or sad. Often, they don't realize what they are saying so it is better to listen to hear them out and then try to figure out what they need. It doesn't help to jump to conclusions when you engage with them."

Hearing Binny speak about her life, her study, the pleasure she feels in engaging with students and the world at large, her prioritizing her health over over-committing herself, I felt that she had found her own balance. It was the Brahma Kumaris for Binny. It could be any other path for you. You have to figure out what works best for you. But the message this chapter tries to relay is keep your balance whatever path you choose. Here I am reminded of my very spiritual but light in spirit friend David. He says a useful sign of spiritual intelligence is you should come across as very normal! As an example, he said post-retirement he has dedicated his life to practicing and teaching spirituality but he still keeps up with the score of most popular sports! Point taken, David.

So, do what you need to do to get on with life. Fulfill your duty to yourself and those you are responsible for. Spirituality applied well should help you and your loved ones enjoy a richer, more meaningful life.

PART SEVEN

What if the whole world became spiritually intelligent? A psychic predicts when it will happen.

I have something to confess. Over the last three decades I have been consulting a psychic by the name of Marilyn, who is also an ordained minister with the Spiritualist Church of Canada.

A friend introduced me to Marilyn soon after I walked out of my marriage of twenty-one years. I was pretty messed up at the time. Back then, I used to visit Marilyn once a year for readings. She lives just outside Toronto with her husband and three children. We would always sit at her kitchen table with a deck of Tarot cards and a cup of tea. Since I adopted a travelling lifestyle, we connect by telephone. I make it a point to connect with her when I am in doubt about a person or a situation.

Marilyn's predictions for me have always come true. Sometimes her timing is off but other than that she is excellent.

I couldn't possibly leave Marilyn out of this book when she has contributed so meaningfully to my life.

Marilyn's take on spiritual intelligence is that it is a sense of awareness that brings wholeness within your being, and that wholeness in turn enhances your quality of life.

I asked Marilyn what the world would be like if everyone on the planet became spiritually intelligent.

"Well, let me first speak of the individual," she said. "I consider myself spiritually aware and I think an outcome of that is how I feel internally. I often say that I am the richest woman on the planet. That is truly how I feel."

"By richest you mean…?" I prompted, wanting greater insight.

"It is not the house I live in. It is not the car I drive. I have what money cannot buy. I have a total sense of serenity within me. I don't know what it is like to be stressed."

I nodded, understanding her perspective.

"If the entire world were spiritually intelligent, at the level of the community, we would see a change in societal priorities," she started.

"Such as," I prompted.

"We would be aware that there is more to life than just indulging ourselves. Money will not be important," she smiled.

"People will have everything that they need," she continued.

"We would no longer live in a male dominated society."

I sat upright at that.

"That's interesting," I said.

She nodded.

"Society would become more conscious of the feminine principal," she said. "Men would see women as equals."

"And how would spiritual intelligence change how we see each other?" I asked.

"We would all belong to one race," said Marilyn.

"Wow," I said.

"Look, right now, we are fighting with borders. As far as humanity goes we aren't spiritually intelligent at all. Borders mean we harbor division in the mind.

"If we were truly spiritually intelligent, we would dissolve our borders and understand that we are all brothers and sisters," she continued. "Just think of how many people and nations presently see refugees. We don't stop to think where they are coming from, the conditions under which they are forced to leave their homes and basic necessities. The stigma they face for being refugees. The challenges they face such as dealing with a new country, a new language, a new climate and all of that. We see them as invaders."

I nodded.

"How would spiritual intelligence change how we see the planet?"

"We would look after the planet. It is the only one we have. Nobody is moving to Mars as yet."

A few lines from John Lennon's Imagine came to my mind...

Imagine there's no countries
It isn't hard to do
Nothing to kill or die for
And no religion, too.
Imagine all the people
Living life in peace
You may say that I'm a dreamer
But I'm not the only one
I hope someday you'll join us
And the world will be as one.

*

"Marilyn, what would it take for entire communities to become spiritually intelligent?"

"For starters, you and I need to become aware and peaceful," she said. Change starts with me."

When I was writing this book my grandson Ben shared a piece of research that he thought would be relevant for my book! Let me share his analysis.

While writing a d'var Torah, an essay based on the weekly portion of the Torah, the first part of the Jewish Bible, Ben had an epiphany about evolution. He discovered that the 'shekel' was a weight measurement in ancient times but when Israel was founded the shekel became a currency, somewhat like the British pound, the Egyptian pound, the Jersey pound and the Lebanese pound evolved from being weight measurements into currencies.

While on the subject of evolution, Ben's imagination was caught by the Aravrit, an experimental font based on the Aravit Arabic font and the Ivrit Hebrew font. The top half of the Aravrit is Arabic, the lower is Hebrew. Ben thought that the Aravrit suggests that nations and people can work together and evolve into more caring people, even if they have been doing otherwise so far.

He surmised, "just as language is evolving we should too. We should become better people and make this world a better place," he wrote me.

"Doing something good can cause a ripple effect even if it is small. When someone does something kind to you, you get an incredible feeling inside that makes you feel great. Let's pass on that feeling to everyone we can by being kind and helping each other. Take the high road. Settle your differences peacefully because fighting will not solve anything."

Marilyn gave me an excellent example of a community coming together to respond to adversity peacefully.

In 2014, the people of a small German town by the name of Wunsiedel, famous for being the burial site of Adolf Hitler's deputy Rudolf Hess, came up with a clever response to the annual neo-Nazi march through the town that has been taking place for decades, an event they disapproved of but had no power to stop.

The people designed a fund-raising initiative tied to the march. Essentially, for every step the right-wing extremists took, local businesses and philanthropists donated ten Euros to a not-for-profit working to counter racism.

The 200 neo-Nazis had two choices when they got to know about the plan. They could go ahead with the march and indirectly donate money to a cause committed to their downfall, or they could cancel their plan. They decided to press on.

So that year, instead of watching the march from a distance, the residents of Wunsiedel cheered on the 200 neo-Nazis as they walked and showered them with rainbow confetti, cleverly thought of because of the symbolism. Neo-Nazis are anti-gay.

The extremists wanted to show power and distinction. Instead of being overwhelmed by negativity, the people chose to respond lovingly and out of forgiveness.

*

I couldn't wait any longer to ask Marilyn this next question.

"It sounds as though spiritual intelligence could bring utopia on earth. Do you really see all this change as really happening?"

"Yes," she said.

"Do you think this will happen gradually or suddenly?"

"I think it will happen gradually."

"When do you see this happening?" How could I not ask a seer that question!

"Right now Pluto is in Capricorn, which is nasty, very, very nasty," explained Marilyn. "It started in 2008. It stays the same until 2024. After that we move into the sign of Aquarius. Aquarius is a unique sign. It could bring in a new awakening, a new revolution of some sort. My fear is where we go with that revolution. Are we going to take the high road or are we going to let the corporate take over?"

"Corporate," I questioned.

"Corporate symbolizes money and greed and unethical practices which are rampant today."

"So do you think we will eventually win over the corporate mindset?"

"By the time Capricorn gets to Pisces, which is in the 2040s, we will have become spiritually aware."

"Ah!" I said. "So it will happen."

What if spirituality doesn't appeal to you?

It is somewhat ironic that of all the definitions and explanations of spiritual intelligence I heard while researching this book, the one person who said, "I don't have a spiritual view of spirituality", was a man of God. I'm talking of none other than Will, who as I've introduced before, is a minister with the Church of Scotland and director of the Center of Theological Inquiry in Princeton NJ, USA.

When I asked Will for his definition of spiritual intelligence, he told me of a Gospel story in the New Testament, of a man who is possessed by demons. Jesus drove out the demons from him and thus healed him. And then Jesus cast out the demons into an abyss.

"And here is the phrase that means everything to me," continued Will. "It says that the man was found 'clothed and in his right mind'."

"Okay," I said, frankly not understanding what Will had meant.

Will must have read my mind because he quickly explained. "I see that as having his dignity restored. As physical creatures, to be clothed means to have your dignity and your social identity and your health and cleanliness restored."

"Ah!" I said.

"We understand how fashion can be destructive but on the other side, it infuses self-respect," he explained. "Particularly for poorer people clothes are very important for their dignity."

I recollected seeing children in Jamaica and India coming out of small huts perfectly turned out in flawlessly ironed, sparkling white clothes, proudly carrying their lunch boxes.

I chuckled and shared that image with Will, saying, "Seeing those kids was always amazing. I wondered how their mothers pulled it off. I never could have."

"To be clothed is an image of dignity but also of individuality," continued Will.

To make his point, he described his grandmother - a working class woman, very house proud. She kept her house clean, like an immaculate palace. He showed me a photograph of her as a young woman in the 1920s. She was a wonderfully dressed flapper.

The photograph made me think of my own preference in clothing. Decades ago showy clothes appealed to me. In those days I used to dress to look attractive. As I found myself, the accent shifted to comfort and to blend in with the surroundings. I no longer sought to impress. The funny thing is, when I became comfortable within myself, I found people got attracted to me, even if for different reasons.

Will gave me another example of an elderly man who had lost his wife and seemed to have come apart. "One day I saw him in town," he said. "He looked smart. I knew he was a grieving widower. But his clothes suggested he was proud and that he had the inner resources to keep living. I thought how brave he was."

I nodded. That made sense. In the Biblical narrative of the man being found clothed and in his right mind, clothes were a metaphor for inner strength, for self-esteem.

I have come to believe that happiness comes from feeling comfortable within yourself, and that can only happen when you understand who you are and where you fit in. Only when you are comfortable with yourself will you think of giving to the people in your life and your community. The world may be too much to say.

"What about 'in his right mind'?" I asked. "How do you interpret that?"

"To be in your right mind does not mean to be bright and brainy. It means to be emotionally and spiritually well. Not terrorized, but with a healthy sense of reality, a sense of your own autonomy as well as interdependence with others, or what we call humility.

"Spiritual intelligence for me would be the pursuit of a way of life that allows people to be in that Biblical image, clothed and in their right mind.

"I think the important thing to understand, Betty, is that spirituality is not a thing in itself but a dimension of human life. We can't live healthy, wholesome lives without it."

Wow! Will's simple statement seemed to encapsulate much of the wisdom I came across while researching this book.

How can you stay calm despite the madness in the world around you? How do you look at a murderer in the eye without hate? How can you take responsibility for your life? How can you do your bit for the environment?

Whether you are of a spiritual bent of mind or not, if you seek to live meaningfully in these times, you need answers to these questions. What's in a name? It is wisdom you can use.

PART EIGHT

Epilogue

I remember being told by Gopi, my inspiration who talked me into doing this project that I would grow spiritually by doing this book. I didn't understand that at all at the outset. I just thought interviewing people would be fun!

Along the way I was taken aback by the openness and selflessness of those I interviewed. They shared so much of their lives and their personal journeys to help you, the reader, find a path of your own.

It would have been impossible for me not to have been touched by their stories.

In working on this project, I have come out of the closet as far as my own spiritual growth is concerned. Today, I say with all honesty that I have travelled to India some twenty-something times since 1991 because I have had my deepest spiritual experiences in that country.

Most of my visits to India have involved stays at the Brahma Kumaris. I know my friends and my children are curious about my relationship with that group. I have met some of the brightest individuals I have known in my life in Mount Abu, the headquarters of the Brahma Kumaris. We have accepted one another with respect and caring, without any attached labels, which has been so refreshing. They have brought meaning to my life that I otherwise never would have had. I always say I am homeless by choice, but thanks to the Brahma Kumaris, I have a number of heart homes around the world.

Some years ago I became aware that God is my protector. Life came full circle. I had been close to the divine during my childhood, then I drifted away and now He is an integral part of my life. What with all of the travelling I do and the situations I get into, planned or not, I would be dead by now if it wasn't for God.

Travel has shown me what a small world we live in. Wherever you go, people for the most part are just trying to live the best life they can, free of violence, sickness and stress, with their loved ones.

When you know God, you open the doors to the values that make life meaningful - honesty, love, kindness, forgiveness and so on. Life doesn't become a rose garden; you still have to work at it. Know yourself and be ready to work on your shortcomings. I have said so in this book and will say it once more as I sign off. Detachment has been one of the most challenging things for me to learn. To love without hanging on, to love without expecting because expectation, the wise say, is spiritual suicide!

At the ripe old age of seventy-six, I realize how lucky I am to have newness in my life. Boredom is not something I do well at all!

Betty

INTERVIEWEES

Binny Sareen, India
Binny Sareen and I became friends during one of my early visits to Mount Abu. She has spent almost all her life in the hill town, her parents having relocated there after being influenced by the spiritual knowledge of the Brahma Kumaris, a practice Binny took to as a child. Binny has worked towards a doctoral degree in spirituality in recent years, something she is proud to have accomplished.

Briony Bax, UK
Briony Bax is a trained actress who works as the editor of Ambit, a British literary and arts magazine with a global audience. Briony and I struck up a friendship about ten years ago. I admire her for founding and successfully running a charity supporting orphans in Kenya, Africa.

Charlie Hogg, Australia
Charlie Hogg is director of the Brahma Kumaris, Australia. Charlie was a wonderful host when I spent a month in Australia after embarking on my wandering lifestyle.

Claire Dunphy, Indonesia
Claire Dunphy is one of my oldest friends, in terms of age, I mean. She is now going strong in her eighties. When I first met her on a mountain top in Australia in the early nineties, she was chanting and waving feathers in front of graves in the rocks. I thought she was quite mad! Anyway, we spent a week together in the bush (Australian for outdoors away from cities) and really clicked. Despite her maverick ways, she is one of the wisest souls I know who really does walk the talk. Claire recently published a book on her life, Becoming Earthwoman: Thank You Notes from a Grateful Guest.

David Goodman, UK

David Goodman worked as a children's dentist until he retired. Now he indulges his love for meditation and sports. I first met David in 1990 on my maiden visit to India as a guest of the Brahma Kumaris, a socio-spiritual organization he is associated with.

Devindree Pillay, South Africa

Devindree Pillay is a thoughtful woman from Durban, South Africa. She is a qualified occupational therapist with her own business.

Elisabeth Angeby Hesslefors, Sweden

Elisabeth Angeby Hesslefors retired as a senior lecturer at the University of Gothenburg in 2011 after a lifetime of teaching and travelling. I was introduced to her at a meditation retreat in India through her husband Ragnar Angeby, a former diplomat with the Swedish Ministry of Foreign Affairs, Sweden's ambassador to Romania in the mid nineties, and current advisor to the Folke Bernadotte Academy, a Swedish agency for peace, security and development. Elisabeth and I became friends through our chats on life.

Eric Le Reste, Canada

Eric Le Reste is a media person based out of Montreal. He makes documentaries for the Canadian Broadcasting Corporation. He also runs the Montreal centre of the Brahma Kumaris, and coordinates the activities of this organization in Canada. I think of Eric as one of my best friends. We have known one another for thirty years, and make it a point to catch up every year.

Glynis German, Majorca

Glynis German works as a wedding celebrant on the island of Majorca. She also hosts a radio show (Just Glynis) and runs a Death Café (if you please) where people come together to discuss death (truly innovative). We met when I visited Majorca about five years ago and have kept in touch.

Gopi Patel, UK & Greece

Gopi Patel is a youngish, evolved woman of Indian origin, raised in

Africa and the UK, who has of late been travelling the world teaching Raja Yoga meditation. Gopi is the one who set me on this project, I must admit. At the time, she was teaching Raj Yoga meditation in Athens, Greece.

Dadi Janki, India

I look upon Dadi Janki, the present head of the Brahma Kumaris, as my spiritual mentor. I knew she was special from the moment I first met her in 1989, in Canada. Dadi was seventy-four at the time, I was forty-six. When I embarked on my travelling lifestyle at the age of seventy, I asked Dadi for her blessing and also for permission to visit certain centers of the Brahma Kumaris. She asked if I thought seventy was too old to start a travelling lifestyle. I said no. She just looked at me, waved her hand and said go. I took that as my blessing and permission! Dadi was 103 years old when I met her last year to ask for her definition of spiritual intelligence, which was simple but deep, 'inner light'.

Jayanti Kirpalani, UK

Jayanti Kirpalani is European Director of the Brahma Kumaris. She has been travelling the world to share ideas on spirituality since forty years. I've known her for the last three decades. She is globally respected for her spirituality. Jayanti has represented the Brahma Kumaris at the United Nations. In 2018, she was asked to lead meditation at Davos, the annual meeting of the World Economic Forum, an event that brings together the who's who of the political and business world and of late, environment thought leaders. In recent years, Jayanti has been speaking widely on climate change. She has led the Brahma Kumaris delegation to climate change conferences of the United Nations.

Jenny Kartupelis, UK

Jenny Kartupelis is a good friend based in Cambridge, UK, who has worked for years for the World Congress of Faiths as the strategy and development officer. She was previously the director (and a co-founder) of the East of England Faiths Council for over a decade, an organization working with the local and national government to promote faith in society and interfaith in the region. In 2010, Jenny was awarded the MBE (member of the Most Excellent Order of the British Empire, a British order of chivalry) for her services to interfaith.

Judy Buddle, Canada

Judy Buddle was my neighbor when my children were young. She is a very humane person. Judy had ten children, many adopted from different countries. She was a huge support to me when my daughter Terri was seriously sick in the hospital and my elder daughter Jody needed to be looked after.

Judy Johnson, Canada

Judy Johnson is a qualified and successful facilitator and specialist in organizational development, based in Canada. She was one of my mentors for this book project. She has been practicing Raja Yoga meditation since many years.

Kathy Barrett, USA

Kathy Barrett and I have been friends since 2012. We were introduced by a common acquaintance and thereafter she attended the first Spirit of Humanity forum in Iceland as my guest. Kathy is a successful writer living in Woodstock, a wooded town in upstate New York best known for the famous music festival held near it in 1969. What strikes me most about her is her natural spirituality. She is spiritual without being part of any formal spiritual group.

Ken O'Donnell, Brazil

Ken O'Donnell is an Australian author and consultant living in Brazil. He is a senior Raja Yoga meditation practitioner with the Brahma Kumaris and coordinates their thirty or so centers in South America. Ken started his career as an industrial chemist and has since worked in quality control, processes, organizational development and leadership development. Over five decades, he has delivered over a thousand talks in Australia, India, USA, Europe and Latin America on stress management, positive consciousness, motivation, conflict resolution and other subjects. When I was researching this project, I came across a Wiki entry on spiritual intelligence. It told me that in 1997, Ken had introduced the term 'spiritual intelligence' in his Portuguese book Endoquality, a term symbolizing the emotional and spiritual dimensions of human beings in organizations. Just goes to show how ahead of the time he was in his thinking.

Manuela Stoerzer, Spain

Manuela Stoerzer is a special friend. She is hip, she is beautiful and that is why she is a model. Manuela is also a life coach. She describes herself as Europe's first walking coach. Manuela enjoys travelling the world and has authored several books in English and German.

Margaret Trudeau, Canada

Margaret Trudeau is widely known for being the mother of Justin Trudeau, the present Canadian prime minister. However, when I first met her in the early eighties, she was better known for being a former first lady. Margaret had three children with Pierre Elliott Trudeau, the prime minister of Canada at the time. In her own right, Margaret is an accomplished author, actress, photographer, former television talk show hostess and a social advocate for people with bipolar disorder, a condition she has long suffered from.

Marie-Lise How Fok Cheung, Mauritius

I have known Marie-Lise How Fok Cheung for about five years. When we first met, Marie-Lise was the senior chief executive of the ministry of health in Mauritius, a very senior position where she had about 13,000 people working under her. She came across as self assured, very capable and with a strong value system. Marie-Lise has since retired. We are close friends.

Marilyn Mazzotta, Canada

Marilyn Mazzotta is a psychic, who is also an ordained minister with the Spiritualist Church of Canada. A friend introduced me to Marilyn soon after I walked out of my marriage of twenty-one years. I was pretty messed up at the time. Back then, I used to visit Marilyn once a year for readings. Since I adopted a travelling lifestyle, we connect by telephone. She has made very valuable contributions to my life.

Marta Matarin, Spain

Marta Matarin is a lovely lady in her forties. She has been coordinating the teaching centre of the Brahma Kumaris in Barcelona for seventeen years. Marta has had a very deep, close relationship with God since she was a child.

Mathilde Sergeant, India

Mathilde Sergeant is of Dutch origin. She was a missionary in her early adulthood. Today, she is a Raja Yoga meditation practitioner and a qualified nurse with a lifetime of nursing experience. I have known Mathilde almost since she relocated permanently to India from the Netherlands in the mid nineties. She is a most valued friend.

Michael Levine, USA

Michael Levine and I go back a long way. We met at Esalon, a spiritual retreat centre in California about thirty-five years ago. He is a true friend. He is a retired professor of political science. He lives in California, USA.

Nancy Stewart, UK

Nancy Stewart and I made friends on one of my many visits to Mount Abu. Nancy is Scottish. She had a rough personal life and only found fulfillment and true happiness after she found God. She is a qualified nurse and enjoyed a successful career before she retired.

Neville Hodgkinson, UK

Neville Hodgkinson is a medical and science writer, who I first met in the early nineties, in UK, just prior to my first visit to India. He is a long-time practitioner of Raja Yoga meditation and a good friend.

Brahma Kumar Nirwair, India

Brahma Kumar Nirwair is one of the very senior members of the Brahma Kumaris in its Mount Abu headquarters. He has been practicing meditation since sixty years; I've known him for thirty years. I can honestly say he is the most gracious man I've ever known.

Dr Partap Midha, India

Dr Partap Midha is medical director of J Watumull Global Hospital & Research Centre, a medium size hospital in Mount Abu, Rajasthan, India.

He has led the hospital since its inception in 1991. I first met Dr Partap during one of my visits to Mount Abu soon after the hospital had started operations. He has been associated with the Brahma Kumaris since he was in his late teens. I am honored to call him my friend.

Pilar Quera, Spain
Pilar Quera is a Raja Yoga meditation teacher based in Barcelona, who I befriended many years ago when I attended a retreat in Spain.

Prue Chambers, Canada
Prue Chambers is an old friend of mine. She is a long time high Anglican minister.

Colonel Raj Pawah, India
Colonel Raj Pawah is a former military man, an engineer and motivational speaker with a keen interest in spirituality, who I met while working on this project. We got talking about spiritual intelligence and it was interesting to hear him say that differences in individual perception are the root cause of every problem in this world.

Samuel Kimbriel, UK & USA
Samuel Kimbriel is an incredibly bright young philosopher. He runs high level think tanks in Washington and the west coast of USA. He is an incredibly wise and humble young man. I believe Samuel has a lot to give to the world and I am sure he will leave his mark in due course. Here's a confession - I am in awe of Samuel! How can someone be so evolved in his early thirties?

Sandra Slovenc Vojvodic, Croatia
Sandra Slovenc Vojvodic is a businesswoman, family person and also the coordinator of the Raja Yoga meditation centre in Zagreb. Sandra is a very beautiful, stylish young woman. She is very clear about where she has been and where she needs to go.

Savi Balladin, Canada
Savi Balladin coordinates the Toronto chapter of the Brahma Kumaris, a meditation centre I visit whenever I am in town. Savi and her colleague run the place very efficiently. Savi is someone I care for and trust.

Seeta, Rwanda

Seeta is a Mauritian settled in Kigali, Rwanda since 2007. She runs the Raja Yoga meditation centre and commands great respect from the community she lives in. I got to know her when I visited the country to see the Genocide Museum. I found her the epitome of humility and the perfect host.

Shivani Verma, India

Shivani Verma is a Raja Yoga meditation teacher who I call the bright star of the Brahma Kumaris for delivering talks around the world and for her global following. I first heard about her from a Canadian friend who used to watch her TV show! I have had the privilege of meeting her and she is the personification of humility. I must also say I have always been impressed with the speed at which she answers emails - as if she has all the time in the world!

Upkar Arora, Canada

Upkar Arora is a successful business man, a family man and a deep thinker, who I call a friend. We met around fifteen years ago when we both sat on the board of an art gallery in Toronto, where he lives. We have stayed in touch since, catching up whenever I am in the city.

William Storrar, UK and USA

William Storrar is a minister of the Church of Scotland and director of the Center of Theological Inquiry in Princeton NJ, USA. I first met Will, as his friends call him, about five years ago at a Spirit of Humanity forum in Iceland. He invited me to attend a residential conference at Windsor Castle, which was an amazing experience, and later hosted me when I visited Scotland.

Yogesh Sharda, Turkey

Yogesh Sharda is a teacher and practitioner of Raja Yoga meditation based out of Turkey. Yogesh started to meditate when he was all of nine years old. His parents introduced him to meditation and he took to it naturally, waking up early morning to exercise his mind. He is a lovely soul, very deep and methodical.

www.ingramcontent.com/pod-product-compliance
Lightning Source LLC
La Vergne TN
LVHW041152080426
835511LV00006B/569